A LOVE SURPASSING KNOWLEDGE

In thanksgiving to God
for the saintly life of

Eric Symes Abbott, KCVO

1906–1983

successively

Warden of Lincoln Theological College
Dean of King's College, London
Warden of Keble College, Oxford
Dean of Westminster

and for his distinguished pastoral ministry to so many,
both lay and ordained, as a spiritual counsellor,
friend and 'pastor pastorum'.

A LOVE
SURPASSING
KNOWLEDGE

The Spirituality of
EDWARD KING

MICHAEL MARSHALL

GRACEWING

First published in England in 2023
by
Gracewing
2 Southern Avenue
Leominster
Herefordshire HR6 0QF
United Kingdom
www.gracewing.co.uk

ISBN 978 085244 990 5

Cover design by Bernardita Peña Hurtado

Front cover image:
Bishop King in a photograph by Samuel Walker,
published in September 1889, when King was aged 59
© *National Portrait Gallery*

Typeset by Word and Page, Chester, UK

CONTENTS

FOREWORD

When you are ordained as deacon and priest in the Church of England there is always a retreat before the ordination service itself. Organised by the diocese, a wise and experienced priest (though sometimes a lay person) is invited to lead the ordinands through their spiritual paces. The last few days before ordination are given to prayer and reflection. It is considered vital.

But this doesn't happen when you are ordained as a bishop. If there is a retreat, it is something you have to organise yourself. Perhaps it is the view that if you're going to be a bishop you've already reached such a spiritual maturity as to render this sort of thing superfluous. But I doubt it. Of all disciples of Christ, bishops may well be in the greatest spiritual need. Following the one who was a servant to all, who carried a towel of service and who was nailed to a cross, as bishops we find ourselves placed on a throne. That seat must become the seat of teaching, a footstall for service, a place to kneel as well as sit.

So, when I was called to be a bishop in God's church 18 years ago, I took myself off on retreat, staying with the sisters at Wantage. And for a guide I took with me the Spiritual Letters of Edward King, that humble, wise and godly pastor whose spirituality you can discover here, in his own words, lovingly

put together by Michael Marshall one of the bishops
who officiated at my ordination as a deacon thirty-
eight years ago.

Many of the letters are to the same person, an
ordinand and then a priest whom Edward King
corresponded with over many years. Early on in
the correspondence he simply writes, 'I am trying
to learn what I have often said, "Thy will be done"'
(*Spiritual Letters of Edward King*, ed. B. W. Randolph,
Mowbray, 1910, p. 2).

This, for me, sums up much of what you will find
in this beautiful and helpful book: a source of profound spiritual wisdom flowing from a profound
humility. It is about alignment of life – the alignment
of our lives with the life of God as God comes to us
in Jesus Christ.

Many of the letters are to the bereaved. Edward
King often says that he doesn't have the words to say
and despairs that he is not able to offer more help.
And yet his words are so very helpful, because they
demonstrate a presence and a tenacious faithfulness,
a commitment to know God and to be known.

Consequently, some of the things I read in that
book on that retreat eighteen years ago have become
the touchstone of my ministry as a bishop. They have
shaped how I have tried to be a pastor and evangelist
to the people I have served.

'It is better to be over charitable than overstrict',
writes King (*ibid.*, p. 86).

'What we want is more Christlike Christians' (*ibid.*,
p. 108).

And perhaps hardest of all, 'Only by breaking your poor heart into pieces over and over again can you hope to make (people) begin to think of believing that there is such a thing as love' (*ibid.*, p. 115).

King's words can help us today. Help our hearts.

'Christ is our example, and Christ is our life', says King in one of his Easter sermons quoted later in this book.

This emphasis on a Christ-centred spirituality, rooted in the sacraments of the church, the reading of scripture, and personal prayer was fundamental to King's daily life. He believed, and it was his desire, that the clergy he served could live lives of sanctification; that their holiness of life could be the very best service to the world.

My prayer has been the same, though my personal example falls well short of the mark. But Michael Marshall, himself such an important, godly and inspirational preacher and teacher in the Church of England, leads us to King's humble, simple and Christ-like spirituality. He helps us understand it and enables it to speak afresh, a timely word of grace and challenge for the Church today and of our need to be rooted in Christ. For to be spiritual, says King, simply means having God at the centre.

And that phrase, 'Christlike Christians', appears in his writings many times. Moreover, it finds an echo in the Church of England's current hope, calling for a spiritual and theological renewal of our life in Christ, for as we come out of the horrors and privations of Covid and face enormous spiritual, material, economic and environmental challenge, we are called to be a Church that is centred on and shaped by Jesus Christ. This begins with personal discipleship and prayer and the nurturing of those spiritual disciplines that in turn nurture humble hearts.

We see this in Edward King. We can read about it here, both a challenge and an encouragement for our discipleship.

Turning to Edward King for succour and guidance will help us to be Christlike Christians in a Christlike Church.

+ Stephen Ebor
Epiphany, 2023

INTRODUCTION

Nothing less than a form of genius

Edward King, born on 29 December 1829, was the second son of Walker King, Canon and Archdeacon of Rochester, and Rector of Stone, in Kent. As a child, Edward was less sturdy in health than his older brother and consequently was not sent away for his early schooling. In his early years he was taught at home, first by his father and subsequently by his father's curate, the Rev'd John Day, whom he later followed to Ellesmere, where Day, as rector of the parish, set up a small school.

In February 1848, King matriculated at Oriel College, Oxford, formerly the centre of the Tractarian founding fathers (the likes of Pusey, Keble and Newman), of the Oxford Movement, or the Catholic revival in the Church of England. It was during those years that, along with his studies, he continued to practise the disciplines of a lively Christian faith along Tractarian lines, and such as he had previously learned from his saintly mentor, John Day.

He graduated in 1851, although, and again for reasons of health, he had not read for an honours degree, so that in the words of the great contemporary scholar, Dr Brightman, who, later in life, knew King well:

Intellectually he has sometimes been depreciated, perhaps because he won no academic distinctions. But those who knew him well will perhaps think that he was among the most intellectual persons they have ever met; only, as was perhaps the case with St Anselm, to whom he has been compared, his intelligence was so much a part of his character, so wholly himself that it might easily escape notice in the simplicity and charm of his personality.[1]

After graduating, he took a break with an extended visit to Palestine, before being ordained deacon in 1854 and priest the following year by Samuel Wilberforce, Bishop of Oxford. For the following four years he served as curate to Edward Elton, vicar of Wheatley, a couple of miles or so from the newly founded Theological College of Cuddesdon. It was in those early days at Wheatley that his remarkable pastoral gifts and influence became evident especially with the unruly boys and youths of the village — pastoral gifts which developed into what Canon Liddon was later to describe as 'nothing less than a form of genius'.

Clearly Bishop Wilberforce had observed those gifts from the earliest days, and it was such gifts that prompted him to appoint the young King, first as Chaplain and subsequently, in early 1863, as principal of his recently founded College at Cuddesdon.

It was especially during those same Cuddesdon years as principal that King's unique gifts and influence matured: his winsome personality, authentic piety and remarkable gifts for love and friendship as a teacher and pastor blossomed in training the many ordinands in his care to be, in the words of Rowan Williams, 'pastorally, theologically and humanly competent at a different level of "professionalism" from what had been so widely taken for granted before'.[2]

The formative impact of King's principalship on his students had clearly come to the attention of Gladstone, whose own son Stephen had fallen under the influence of King during his training at Cuddesdon, and, in 1873, Gladstone nominated him to the Queen as the second occupant of the recently founded Chair of Pastoral Theology at Oxford.

For King, pastoral theology required the double grip of both a profound knowledge of theology and spirituality, but also an equally matched awareness of the human condition, head and heart, and all this at a time when the study of psychology was only in its infancy. For King, theology, spirituality and pastoral theology were all of a piece, communicated to his many students preparing for ordination not only from books and lectures, but also from his own seasoned experience in dealing with the souls and lives of men and women, who increasingly sought him out as a spiritual counsellor. 'King', says Russell, his earliest biographer, 'treated pastoral theology as the systematic inculcation, not of abstract theories, however venerable, but of lessons practically learnt in pastoral intercourse with the poor, the tempted and the perplexed . . . His power of sympathy amounted to genius, and gave him an almost supernatural insight into human hearts.'[3]

By 1885, King had become a name and well-known figure both in the Church at large as well as the University, so that when Bishop Christopher Wordsworth, the nephew of the poet, resigned the See of Lincoln for reasons of ill-health, once again it was Gladstone who nominated King to the Queen to fill the vacancy, where, as teacher, pastor and bishop, King flourished for the following twenty five-years until his death, at the age of eighty, in 1910. It was during those same years as bishop that, in the words of Canon Ollard, King became 'one of the post potent religious forces in England', occupying 'a position few English clergymen have attained'.

As this book, serving as something of a sequel to the recently published large biography of Edward King,[4] seeks to demonstrate, King's immense transformative influence was resourced not only from his considerable scholarship, but also from a deep inner life of the Spirit, which influenced the lives of hundreds of clergy for the next generation, many of whom in turn became, bishops, spiritual leaders and heads of Theological Colleges, handing on what they had first received from the teaching and spiritual genius of one who, both during his lifetime as well as subsequently, was and continues to be hailed as a saint.

Although for a very different Church and a very different world, nevertheless there is an urgent need to revisit King so that the spiritual revival in which he played such a demonstrably significant role may challenge and benefit the Church today. As in King's day, the outward structures of the Church—indeed of all the Churches—unquestionably will require to be reconfigured together with a strategic redeployment of the clergy, and yet that in itself was, and is, not enough, either then or now. In King's own words: 'Organization does not produce life, though life may produce organization: the secret of the power is the life.'[5] It is a renewed commitment to the power of that inner life of the Spirit, the root and source of all new life, both taught and caught by clergy and laity alike, which is so urgently needed, as in King's day, and without which all reform and reorganisation will not be effective. It is to that same inner life of the Spirit so clearly evidenced in Edward King, pastor, teacher, bishop, and saint, for which this book seeks to encourage a renewed exploration.

1

Spiritual Renewal and the Church Today

The spiritual life is the life which is controlled and ruled by the Spirit of God and lived in his power.[1]

'Edward King matters', Rowan Williams comments, 'because he helped to restore its soul to the nineteenth century Church of England, as did so many who were inspired or trained by him for a new kind of ministry among the needy and marginal.'[2] The writing of a book which purports to explore the 'spirituality' of one of whom such a claim could be made must surely raise the question: 'What possible relevance could the inner spiritual life of a nineteenth century bishop—however saintly—have for such a vastly different Church and world some two hundred years later?' In order to do justice to that question, we need to set King's distinctive contribution to the spiritual renewal of the Church in the context of the age in which he lived and ministered

King was born in what history retrospectively records as being the 'Age of Reform' when many were agitating for radical reform, not only of Parliament, and the Universities of Oxford and Cambridge but also, and to no lesser extent, the Established Church. Equally vociferous, however, were many, as always at such times, who stubbornly resisted change or who, at least, questioned by what authority and by whom any such reforms should be undertaken.

King's lasting importance and relevance, however, lies neither at the level of his organizational skills compared with the likes of Bishop Wilberforce or the 'meddlesome' Bishop Blomfield of London, nor with regard to the massive intellectual and theological contributions of the founding Fathers of the Oxford Movement of the likes of Pusey, Newman and Keble. King's contribution to the reform and renewal of the Church was of a different order, as this study seeks to show.

King, like Wesley in the previous century, perceived how what Wesley had termed 'Conventional Christianity' was no longer effective to meet the challenges of the new age, when many were questioning the very foundations of the Christian faith.

> I have ventured to speak of the danger of stopping short of that true union with God in Christ, which, as Christians should be ours. I have suggested that such a warning may be needed now, when new forces are developing around us, and producing ways of life, and a conventional Christianity which in some ways it is difficult to reconcile with the natural interpretation of the Gospel and other parts of Revelation.[3]

At every level—whether Darwin with his *Origin of Species* or the historical and literary criticism of the Bible coming out of Germany, championed even by some leading figures within the hierarchy of the Church itself—all this together and so much more had shaken and undermined the very foundations of the authority, ministry and mission of the Church of England.

In the words of the psalmist: 'When the foundations are being destroyed, what are the righteous to do?' (Psalm 11:3). For King, at such a time, as for Wesley in the previous century, the answer was clear—dig for those deeper foundations which are indestructible, and such was the contribution of the radical Edward King—teacher, pastor, bishop and widely acclaimed saint. Others trimmed the branches of the 'vine' of the Lord's vineyard, so to speak, but King, like Wesley before him, went for the root of the matter, namely the inner life of the Spirit and the source of all life—the indwelling Spirit of the Risen, Ascended and Glorified Christ. It was the sap drawn from such deep roots of that inner life of the Spirit which, both during King's lifetime as well as in the following century, bore the fruits of a renewed and empowered ministry and a far-reaching mission, not only in the Church of England, but further afield in the emerging Anglican Communion.

It is in something of that context as outlined above, that the words of Rowan Williams can be confidently reaffirmed with reference to King's importance in restoring, as Williams claims, 'the soul to the nineteenth century Church of England', and hopefully, goes some way towards justifying this exploration into King's spirituality and inner life which was so formative in revitalizing the Church in his own day and subsequently.

SPIRITUALITY AND
THE INNER LIFE IN THE SPIRIT

It is the conviction that a similar radical renewal of the inner life of the Spirit, analogous to that to which King had recalled the Church in his day, is needed also for today's Church, indeed for all the Churches, that has encouraged the publication of this book.

> There has been a remarkable growth of interest in the general area of spirituality. A resurgent cynicism concerning the value of material possessions has led to much greater attention being paid to the spiritual dimensions of life. A growing body of evidence suggests that personal spirituality has a positive therapeutic effect on individuals, pointing to an increasing recognition of the importance of spirituality to human fulfilment and well-being. Alongside a gradual general decline in the appeal of institutionalized forms of religion in western culture, there has been a clear rise in popular interest in spirituality, including the various forms of Christian spirituality.[4]

So it would seem that, at least on the face of things, 'spirituality' is in again: there's a lot of it about. Along with mindfulness, meditation, yoga and all frequently packaged together with certain dietary disciplines as well as a reawakened care for the planet, that overarching word, 'spirituality', is out in the market place and on the tongues of many who might never have darkened the doors of a church, let alone call themselves Christians: 'I'm not religious, but I am spiritual'. Such is the recurring antiphon on the lips of many, whether born of a cynicism about the prevailing materialism and consumerism in the highly developed countries; the mounting fear concerning climate change, or simply in reaction to the disillusionment with the seeming impotence and irrelevance of the mainstream churches with their, overall, declining congregations.

But what exactly do people mean when they speak of spirituality? It might be worth noting that the very word 'spirituality' is really quite a modern word, and one which incidentally is scarcely, if ever, to be found in any writings we have of Edward King. In fact, Rowan Williams goes as far as to claim that 'if you had asked anybody in the fifteenth or sixteenth century, "Tell me about your spirituality", they would not have had a clue what you were talking about. Spirituality for the Christian is shorthand for "life in the Spirit", for staying alive in Christ',[5] and all the while essentially belonging to and nurtured in, a community of faith.

THE PREVAILING CULTURE OF INDIVIDUALISM

Yet, contrary-wise, 'spirituality' for most people, if at all a word in their vocabulary, would not be associated with a community: more usually, in the western prevailing culture of individualism, it would be perceived as belonging to what would be termed their 'private lives'. Yet, such a privatization of spirituality is totally 'incompatible with Christian spirituality. None can possess the Spirit as an individual, but only as a member of the community. When the Spirit blows, the result is never to create good individual Christians, but members of a community. This became fundamental for Christian spirituality in the New Testament and was in direct line with the Old Testament mentality.'[6]

Then again, such a misguided understanding of spirituality leads to a dualistic view of the world—a world and lifestyle divided between the sacred and the secular, spirit versus matter, resulting in a spirituality which 'is widely seen not as a way of living in every sphere, but rather as a sphere in its own right—"the spiritual dimension". The action of God is thus confined within extremely narrow limits. So it is not surprising that such spirituality serves to reinforce, or at least not to disturb, the status quo. In much of the popular literature which has emerged from the spiritual revival of recent years, prayer and meditation are offered as ways of coping with existing reality'—stress, anxiety or loneliness—'not as ways to change it'.[7]

THE SPIRITUAL LIFE

Repeatedly, King emphasizes the importance of a proper understanding of the so-called 'spiritual life' — what it is, and what it most definitely is not.

> It's important that we should have a right idea,
> as far as may be, of what we mean by a spiritual
> life. It does not mean the life of a spirit as distinct
> from the life of the body. Spiritual lives are led
> by ordinary men and women in the discharge of
> the ordinary duties of daily life . . . The spiritual
> man and the carnal man both live in the body,
> both may be engaged in the same business, the
> same trade, the same profession; but with the
> carnal man self is the centre of his life, and his
> own inclinations and desires and interests and
> pleasures are the moving and ruling principles.
> But with the spiritual man, God is the centre
> of his life, God's will the ruling and controlling
> principle. So, we need not go out of this world
> to live spiritual lives, but whilst living in the
> world we must live above it . . . The spiritual life
> is the life which is controlled and ruled by the
> Spirit of God and lived in His power. 'They that
> are of the Spirit, mind the things of the Spirit.'

Yet, although there is nothing dualistic about King's
world view, or privatized about his faith, or perceived as belonging to some kind of 'private sector'
of life, nevertheless instead of 'private' we most certainly need to read 'personal' and 'intimate' as being
the secret of King's relationship with the Christ of
God in times specifically set apart to nurture and
deepen such a personal relationship.

> While then, we need not go out of the world
> and give up our daily duties, we must give
> our minds to God; we must take time daily to
> meet with God, in prayer, in reading His Word,

and meditating on the truths we read. Our care should be that having put on the new man, we may be renewed in knowledge after the image of Him that created us; that, by the help of the Spirit, spiritual understanding, spiritual wisdom, a full knowledge in the things of the Spirit may be an increasing reality to us; that year by year, we may grow in the knowledge of our Lord and Saviour Jesus Christ.[8]

So unquestionably King would have sharply disagreed with such a privatization of the Christian life-style; indeed, he seldom uses the abstract noun 'spirituality' to refer to the inner life of the Spirit. For King, Christian formation and Christian discipleship are realized to their fullest in a community of faith, formed by the Holy Spirit which is precisely why he saw the work of priestly formation as necessarily being formed in the residential life of the community of faith which he so markedly nurtured at Cuddesdon, where, as King expressed it, *'philia* becomes *koinonia'*. 'King had discovered a momentous truth: that the right method of training ordinands was not to drive them by exhortation along preconceived tram-lines: it was to live a worshiping life in community and let the Holy Spirit do the rest.'[9]

ONE INTEGRATED WHOLE

The same was equally true of Christian formation generally, in requiring membership of a community of faith, nurtured by Word and Sacrament and corporate worship, as well as times of personal prayer, and all issuing in the service of the wider community, and specifically, as in King's case, with a particular care and compassion for the poor and the marginalized.

'King's contribution to spirituality, prayer, pastoral care and moral thought helped to build the foundations for the rediscovery of moral, pastoral and doctrinal theology as one integrated whole'.[10] It is that 'one integrated whole' which pervades the whole of King's theology as expressed in his teaching and exemplified in his spirituality, with its striking balance of head and heart, doctrine and devotion, worship and service.

King never wrote a large book on ethics, as initially he had hoped to do on becoming Professor of Pastoral and Moral Theology in 1873, let alone anything vaguely resembling a treatise on systematic theology,– preferring, it would seem, in the words of Fenelon, to 'write on men's hearts'.

Nevertheless, the opening Homily and the three Addresses that he gave on the occasion of the Quiet Day immediately preceding the Lambeth Conference of 1897, when taken together with the three volumes of published sermons, his *Spiritual Letters* and notes from his pastoral lectures offer a remarkable theological foundation, undergirding that spirituality which he both taught and lived. Furthermore, as in his person, it is all of a piece, centred in and intimately related to the risen, ascended and glorified Christ. Throughout it all there is a subtle, yet nevertheless well-articulated, balance and harmony of head and

heart, nature and grace, all alike, firmly rooted and
grounded in a particular tradition—broadly speaking, that of the English school of spirituality. Yet
with King there is always that freedom of the Spirit
to explore, to learn from and be enriched by other
traditions, all generously affording a capacity to
develop and change, as the times require, with new
expressions and outward forms in which the inner
life of the Spirit is experienced and nurtured.

This is perhaps most succinctly expressed in King's
Second Address to the bishops on that Quiet Day
in 1897:

> One seems to find a real and helpful sequence of
> thought in the seven words: Duty—Conscience—
> God—Scripture—Christ—Church—Holy Spirit.
> There is a need of warning others to beware of
> thinking that they can do their duty, without
> recognizing the claims of conscience; and to
> beware of thinking that they will be able to keep
> their conscience as it ought to be kept, without
> the acknowledgement of God, by losing the aid
> of His own revelation, the Bible; to beware of
> thinking that they believe the Bible, unless they
> believe in Christ; to beware of thinking that they
> can partake of Christ with all the fulness that
> may be theirs, except in the way that He has
> appointed through His Church; and finally to
> beware of thinking that they can do all things
> in their natural strength without accepting the
> gift of the Spirit.[11]

On that same occasion, and with notable theological
dexterity, he drives home the point he is attempting
to make for the bishops by considering, as he says,

'these words in their inverse order'. It is as though King realized that seekers start at different 'staging posts' on that inner journey of the Spirit to explore the fullness of life in Christ: some perhaps beginning with duty, as in the public-school religion so conspicuously proffered by Arnold and Rugby School at that time. Others are impacted by the Holy Spirit as a kind of 'kick-start' (analogous to falling in love), to their pilgrimage of the heart, prompting and motivating a life-long journey of ever broadening and deepening discipleship. Yet in order to appropriate that fullness and abundance of new life which Christ came to bring, King insists that at least, all seven ingredients are needed. So he continues to spell out the seven 'map-references' for that inner pilgrimage of the heart, but in reverse order so as to demonstrate how interdependently and inextricably they are interwoven like a seamless garment in the inner life of the Spirit—that life which King so manifestly exemplified in his own person.

It is useful to caution some against thinking that they are living in the *Spirit* unless they are willing to be guided by the *Church*. It is needful to caution some to beware of trusting their zeal for the *Church*, unless they really look to *Christ*—to the example of His life, the reality of forgiveness through the atoning virtue of His death, and the power of His resurrection; to beware of thinking that they will be able to keep their hold on Christ unless they search the *Scriptures* with the view of coming nearer to Him, and of growing in grace and in the

> knowledge of our Lord and Saviour Jesus Christ;
> to beware of trusting to a mere knowledge of
> the Scriptures unless they set *God* always before
> them, obeying their *conscience* as His voice, and
> showing their obedience by doing their daily
> *duty*, however humble it may be.[12]

But this exposition by King of ascetical theology
and the spiritual life or the inner life of the Spirit
had clearly been unfolding long before the Lambeth
Addresses of 1897. In fact we find a very similar outline in some Lent Retreat Addresses given as early
as 1883 at St Mary Magdalene's, Paddington, during
King's time in Oxford as professor. Here as later, the
seven ingredients all belong together as a package
deal, where once again King cautions any picking
and choosing from personal, let alone denomina-
tional, preference, and while again defying any order
of priority:

> Beware of trying to live a moral life without God,
> or trying to believe in God without the help of
> revelation, or trying to accept the Bible without
> Christ, or trying to accept Christ without the
> Church he has appointed, or trying to accept
> the Church without the sacraments.[13]

All this taken together, from what we know of
King's teaching suggests some kind of road map
for the Christian life of discipleship, and in many
ways will form the outline of this book's study into
King's spirituality, life and ministry which, as Rowan
Williams suggests, 'helped to restore its soul to the
nineteenth century Church of England'.

This, it would seem, is the nearest we might get with King to any kind of systematic theology, or any major work on the inner life of the Spirit, and yet, as he himself pleaded to the assembled bishops at Lambeth, such interrelated and interdependent building blocks, could help to 'preserve a living relation to truth' as well as giving 'unity and power to the life'[14] of the Spirit. It was that 'unity and power to life' and 'a living relation to truth' experienced as a personal relationship with the One who claimed to be the Truth, that gave authority to his teaching and preaching, and all alike resourced by the indwelling Spirit of the risen, ascended and glorified Christ, nurtured by Word and Sacrament: it is precisely these several building blocks which will form the structure of this whole study.

A LOVE SURPASSING KNOWLEDGE

It is by taking together all the interrelated ingredients outlined as above by King that, in King's words, give 'a living relation to the truth' and 'unity and power to the Christian life': in a word holiness of life. It was holiness of life which for King was the point of it all by keeping, in the words of that same Lambeth Address, our 'hold on Christ, with the view of coming nearer to Him, and of growing in grace and in the knowledge of our Lord and Saviour Jesus Christ'.

King's Christology is thoroughly Pauline and especially as in the three later letters, attributed to

Paul—Colossians, Philippians and Ephesians. In his pastoral lectures, King stresses the importance of these three letters as giving a 'strong view of St Paul's Christology and of the grandeur of the revelation of Christ'.[15] Central to King's spirituality is the person of Christ—the indwelling Christ. The Holy Spirit, the Scriptures, the Sacraments of the Church are resources pointing us, beyond themselves and 'drawing' us so that we may grow 'in grace and in the knowledge of our Lord and Saviour Jesus Christ'. However, with King in particular , the word 'knowledge', as we shall find throughout this study, conveys so much more than the knowledge of information about an object or a person—as in French, *savoir* knowledge. No, this is so much more than that. It is the knowledge of a personal and intimate relationship, as in French, *connaître* – or indeed as frequently in the Old Testament, where a man 'knowing' a woman or vice versa, means the intimacy of sexual intercourse.

So when Jesus says, 'This is eternal life, to *know* the Father and him whom he sent' (John 17:3), there is a real sense in which it signifies the end and purpose of all religion, inviting as it does, a relationship, communion and union as intimate as the bond of marriage and deep friendship, as also in a similar sense, when Jesus, on the eve of his crucifixion, says to his anxious disciples: 'I no longer call you servants, I call you my friends' (John 15:15). And again, when Jesus says 'I am the Way, the Truth and the Life' (John 14:6): the fullness of truth who Jesus is, is so much more than information learned in the abstract from books and primarily addressed to the reason. The Way, the Truth and the Life are known by experience and from within a relationship with the One who claimed to be all three (as He is light, life and love), all alike indicating that real, abundant, eternal life are experienced essentially as life in relationship, while contrary-wise the isolation from the source or root, implied as 'private life', like a cut-flower existence, signifies death.

In one of his annual letters to the nurses of the Guild of St Barnabas, King reiterates the importance of this intimate union with Christ, apprehended from experience: 'We know "the love of Christ which surpasses knowledge"; and all this is for us Christians not as a mere picture, or figure of speech, for us to look at or read about as something external to us; but all this is *in* us because we are in Christ.'[16]

And again, in the course of one of those Lenten addresses referred to earlier:

> Oh, I know it, I know it; it is the great central joy of my life! I can see it, I can feel it, the love of Jesus for me, for *my* soul. He died for me. He gave his very *life for* me. And if our hearts are really opened to Him, *anything* may be possible to us.[17]

Little wonder that Scott Holland, in his characteristic euphoria, on hearing of King's appointment to Lincoln, burst out in a letter to King: 'It shall be a Bishopric of Love—"The Love of God behind, and above, and about you! The Love of the Blessed Spirit, alive with good cheer within! The Love of the Poor shining out from you."[18]

This, for King, is the foundation on which he built his whole life and from which everything else derives its significance and purpose—the very end (*telos*) for which we were created. Yet, it is not, as it might first appear, that individualistic piety or an elitist mysticism, frequently caricatured as being 'so heavenly minded, as to be of no earthy use'. On the contrary, concerns for justice, social action and the love of neighbour are rightly perceived as being the second commandment, yet always and inextricably resourced and overflowing from the love of God as in the first and great Commandment. With typical simplicity King spells this out:

> We shall not rise to the height of heaven if we have not the Love of God, and we shall not rise to the height of heaven if we have not the love of our neighbour. It must be the double stroke of the *two* wings, the love of God and the love of neighbour. No wild religious fanaticism, which makes us careless as to our neighbour's needs, will carry us up to the God who is Love. No mere philanthropy or doing kind things will purify our souls, and make us fit to rise into the Presence of Him before whom the angels veil their faces. No! . . . if we want to rise to heaven, it must be by the beat of the *two* wings, the love of God and the love of our neighbour.[19]

THE NATURE OF HOLINESS

Although, even during his lifetime, many spoke of King, as 'the holy Bishop of Lincoln' who 'is adored'[20] by his people, there was never anything self-conscious in King which sought to parade his manner of life or, as in the words of the Collect for King's Commemoration on 8 March, seeking to 'draw' people to himself. It is true, as we shall see later in more detail, that King, as with all the Tractarians, exhorted others, notably the clergy and ordinands, to aim at that fullness of life which would be spoken of as holiness, and which thereby would authenticate the message which the person of the messenger first embodied in his or her own lifestyle. Yet, that outward and visible form must derive its attraction from within and from a hidden and inner life-force constantly renewed and reinvigorated from the various elements of a spirituality such as that outlined above and further developed in the following chapters.

'The hope that God's grace could be realized through individual and corporate holiness in such a manner as to evidence the authenticity of the Christian faith served as an important dynamic at the very heart'[21] of the Oxford Movement, and never more so, than with King. Conversely, 'what was most dangerous to faith—most likely to disprove its claims—was inauthentic Christian living'—that 'Conventional Christianity' so deplored by Wesley.

With respect to King, and with particular reference to his spirituality, as in the following chapters, any application of the word 'holiness' to him might imply a diminishment in life, in the senses or a full delight in God's creation, and of course nothing could have been less true of King. On the contrary, as Scott Holland remembered him:

> He grew happier and happier. His eyes twinkled with dauntless merriment: his presence brimmed over with joy. After all the earth was a good place: and heaven would be better still. God be thanked![22]

So, on the contrary, a spirituality leading to holiness of life is, when rightly and fully developed, a far cry from being a diminishment, but rather is a process leading through the narrow way to ever broadening horizons the further we go and the process whereby we become persons in the fullest sense, or 'fully alive' to use the definition of Irenaeus, always beautifully reflecting the light, life and love of the 'glory of God in the face of Jesus Christ' (II Corinthians 4:6). Such was something of what King's contemporaries observed in his outward features, his teaching, preaching and manner of life. Cosmo Gordon Lang wrote of how he had been confirmed by 'that most beautiful, sane and cheerful of saints',[23] and of which Cosmo Gordon Lang spoke so powerfully in Lincoln Cathedral on the fiftieth anniversary of King's consecration as bishop, when he referred to King as being 'the most saintly of men, and the most human of saints'.[24]

AN OPPORTUNITY AND CHALLENGE
FOR THE CHURCH TODAY

Although historical parallels should be heeded with caution as frequently being over simplistic, nevertheless it is not difficult to see how the plight of the Church in our own day, with its apparent irreversible decline numerically of churchgoers, parallels in some ways a similar decline, as in the nineteenth century, and likewise also requiring a spiritual 'rebooting' to recover its soul and inner life, by a return to its roots from which the sap of any new and renewed life is drawn. As in King's day, theology and theologians will have an important part to play in any such renewal together with those who can engage with other disciplines with a lively apologetic. Also, and again as in King's day, this will inevitably involve reorganization and change which, as we consistently see on every front, are never experienced, least of all at the time, as comfortable or popular. It follows that the outward form of the Church as a living organism will continually need to adapt if it is to 'house' fittingly the developing and maturing inner life of the Spirit.

Yet, that in itself, was not enough then, and neither will it be in any age. Rather, it is the hidden, inner life of the Spirit which tailors and fashions the outward form, and which must of priority 'call the tune', for it is from that inner source rather than any outward re-imaging in appearance, which has the eternal drawing power of 'Jesus Christ, the same yesterday, today and forever' (Hebrews 13:8).

So of course, reorganization will always be an element in the renewal and revitalization of any institution, such as was undertaken by the bishops in the nineteenth century and as is presently being undertaken, not only by the bishops of the Church of England, but also by the spiritual leaders in all the Churches in our own day: that will always be a recurring need.

But there must also be an accompanying change of heart in the depths of the inner life of the Spirit in the mystical Body of Christ, not only to accompany any changes in the outward forms of worship, prayer and outreach, but as being prior to them, if the outward transformation is not to be, only little better than cosmetic and skin deep. For there is always the danger, as King was frequently at pains to point out, of 'holding the form of religion, but denying the power of it' (II Timothy 3:5).

The apparent ineffectiveness of all the Churches to convey a meaningful and relevant message, as in Wesley's or King's day, and to engage with the imagination of the prevailing culture leads many, as in former times, to a disillusionment with what both Wesley and King spoke of as 'Conventional Christianity'. It's a religion which has retained all the trappings of the outward form of religion and formularies, but which lacks the power to transform lives let alone to grab the attention and imagination of the culture. Clearly King was not unaware of such a disillusionment in his day, but with characteristic perception he seizes on this very factor, as offering the Church an opportunity to speak into that disillusionment, while at the same time recalling the Church to a deeper faith and a more authentic witness resourced, as for King himself, from a renewed inner life of the Spirit.

In 1908, in his penultimate annual letter to the nurses of the Guild of St Barnabas, King cited a passage from a book he had recently read by the Bishop of Bloemfontein on precisely this matter of 'Disillusionment' — a disillusionment born, as King says, from 'the failure of the things of this world to give satisfaction and meaning to life': yet also a 'disillusionment', which King clearly perceives as being a possible 'starting point of experiential religion', that can do 'more than anything else to give substance and sincerity to faith. The man who finds no satisfaction for his affections or will or intellect in the things of this world turns with a hungry soul to God'.

Yet, here is the challenge in the opportunity which such a disillusionment can afford. 'To him God is to be no mere artistic embellishment of a life whose serious interests are elsewhere; not a conventional ground or justification for the restraint of morality nor a recipient of traditional expressions of homage and respect, not a polite synonym for all that is obscure, mysterious, and unknowable in his surroundings.'

Such a superficial religion will not suffice to counter such disillusionment, King continues, for 'on the contrary, God is to be to him the object on Whom

every power of his nature is bent, the sum and substance of truth, and beauty and goodness, the food
of his soul, the inspiration of his acts, the familiar
Friend and Counsellor of his everyday life, the Master Who has a right to dispose of him as He Will, and
Whose service is perfect freedom.'[25]

A long cry indeed from the 'conventional Christianity' of a merely churchgoing culture which alone,
can never satisfy the hungry soul, let alone withstand
the ever encroaching claims of an atheistic materialism: in any age, something far deeper and far more
radical will always be required.

C. S. Lewis is reputed to have said that he was not
interested in High Church or Low Church; rather,
what was required was 'deep church' — a sentiment
that would doubtlessly be applauded by King himself, who repeatedly spoke of the need for 'simplicity
and depth' when teaching about the Christian life,
discipleship and the inner life of the Spirit.

Could it be that some of the present disenchant-
ment with organized religion and the quest for a
more personalized spirituality, albeit somewhat
misguided, nevertheless constitutes both a similar
opportunity as well as a challenge to the Churches
today, as in the age of King, and especially to the
spiritual leaders of the Churches, calling, as it surely
must, for a redirection of our attention as of first priority, to the inner life of prayer in the Spirit—in short,
nothing less than a rekindling of that flame of sacred
love, which far surpasses the limitations of analytical
knowledge. For without nothing less than this, all

our efforts at reorganization and revitalization are little better than the proverbial reorganization of the deck chairs on the sinking Titanic.

All our right concerns with social justice and good works, are secondary but should issue from an inner transformation of the Spirit, since experience is evidence sufficient that there are no fruits, least of all 'fruits that will last' and bare the test of time, without deeply nurturing roots. Furthermore, the drier the desert, as at the present time, the deeper the roots, as always, will need to be. Only lives, rooted and grounded in Christ, led by the Spirit of the ascended Christ, and the community of faith of whatever size numerically, will fulfil the Church's vocation to be the salt, the light and the leaven, as it is called to be.

We do well to recall that times of spiritual renewal in the history of the Church have occurred when the outward form—the system if you like—in which the spiritual awakening is housed, no longer conveys adequately or appropriately the inner, self-regenerating life of the Spirit. It is at such times—and generally occurring in a particular place, in a particular person or small groups of persons—that the inner life of the Spirit is reasserted until, as with an egg, the outward shell is broken, requiring, indeed demanding, a re-formed and a more suitably tailored outward and visible expression, so as to make visible the hidden life of the Spirit within. In prospect, the whole process is generally misread as decline and death, which in some ways it is, and yet when reviewed retrospectively, it is perceived contrary-wise, as having been a time of renewal and rebirth. Such was the case, when in 1833, Thomas Arnold declared: 'The Church of England as it now stands no human power can save.' And yet, with the benefit of hindsight, we can confidently assert that it was that very same year 1833, which marked the beginning of the Oxford Movement and the beginning of one of the periods of the greatest expansion of the Church, not only in England, but further afield.

With a similar benefit of hindsight, it is abundantly clear that it was precisely that dynamic power of King's own personal inner life of the Spirit, nurtured in worship, bible study, personal prayer and love, expressed in compassion and care for the poor and the marginalized, with its transforming influence on hundreds of clergy and many others of influence in the following generation, which validates that opening comment of Rowan Williams, with which we began, claiming that 'Edward King matters, because he helped to restore its soul to the nineteenth century Church of England, as did so many who were inspired or trained by him'.

For a very different Church, and in a vastly different world, what lessons can we learn from the study which this book seeks to stimulate, that will issue in a similar radical transformation at the present time? That such is needed is surely beyond question.

2

The Victory of Easter
and the New Life of Pentecost

The Resurrection of Christ has placed us now in
a new sphere, in a new life, and brought us into
contact with new forces: the Resurrection of Christ
for us, is a new power.[1]

PREACHING THE VICTORY OF EASTER

It was only a matter of a few weeks after Bishop
Edward King had been enthroned in his cathedral
in Lincoln, when William John Butler was installed
as the new dean of the cathedral. For the following
eleven years, the partnership of bishop and dean
proved to be a happy and fruitful time both for the
cathedral and the diocese. Dean Butler speedily set
to work to refresh and reinvigorate the ministry and
worship of the cathedral and, among many other
innovations, he instituted a popular Sunday evening
service in the nave at six-thirty—a bright, musical
service which proved extremely popular for ordinary working people—and furthermore promptly
invited King to preach at the very first of these.

For the rest of King's years at Lincoln he always preached at that evening service in the nave on Easter Sunday evenings: twelve of these *Easter Sermons* were subsequently published shortly after King's death. It is fortunate that we have most of these Easter sermons precisely because, throughout all of them, there is the consistent reference to the key-stone of the whole Christian theological edifice and its out-workings in Christian spirituality, namely the Paschal Mystery – the Death, Resurrection, Ascension and Glorification and the attendant gift of the Holy Spirit at Pentecost.

For King, the Paschal Mystery is not only a fact of history exemplified once upon a time in the past in the person of Jesus of Nazareth. Nor is it simply the process by which we are saved from our sins and justified—although that is a necessary element in the whole cosmic process of what is termed as accomplishing the redemption of the world: of course, it is all of that and yet so very much more. In the later epistles, attributed to St Paul—Ephesians, Colossians and Philippians, to which King continually refers in his teaching and preaching—the redemptive work of Christ is perceived as of nothing less than cosmic proportions, defying any human time scale, as God's eternal plan, hidden since before the foundation of the world and made visible and tangible in time and space, 'in these last days' in the person of Jesus, the Christ of God. The Paschal Mystery is nothing less than the particularity in time and space enacted and embodied in a particular person of history—Jesus of

Nazareth the Apostle of that eternal plan, whereby God through the process of the incarnation and all that it involved and continues to involve, might reconcile all things and draw all things back to himself, into the heart of God from which everything first derived its origin.

And yet, at the same time and paradoxically from the perspective of the Christian disciple, all this must be owned and appropriated personally in a relationship of intimacy with the Pioneer and Author of that cosmic plan—even the person of Christ himself, who promised through the gift of his own Holy Spirit to be present both personally and corporately in and with his Church until the close of the age.

We are not called to understand fully the ingredients of that process, for it is not that kind of knowledge that the Christian disciple should or needs to seek. Rather, it is the kind of 'knowledge' acquired from nothing less than a relationship of intimacy and 'a love that surpasses knowledge', that is in the usual sense of information. Rather, again as with Paul, the Christian disciple is called to participate as a 'fellow worker' in the continuing process of the Paschal Mystery, both personally and corporately, so that what God in Christ has done *for* us and the whole of creation, might be replicated *in* us, personally but also organically in the living organism of the Church, perceived not simply as an organization, but as the mystical Body of Christ, with Christ as its Head and Christian disciples as living members of the Body, as the hands and feet of the contemporary incarnate Christ in the many diverse cultures of the world, and all that, and so much more, in the here and now.

In that way, and in the language of scripture, the individual Christian is slowly being 'conformed' and transformed into the likeness of Christ's death and resurrection. As Christ was once and for all baptized and plunged into our humanity, thus reclaiming the whole material fabric of creation (for which the New Testament word is *sarx*, translated as 'flesh'), so too may we, by our baptism into his divine life, be raised up together with him in his Body as members of his mystical Body, the Church, with Christ Himself as its head.

King's shorthand language for this whole process, was simply a matter of becoming more 'Christ-like Christians'. Such had been the purpose of his whole ministry, as he said in his last letter to his diocese, a few days before his death: 'My great wish has been to lead you to be more Christ-like Christians . . . In Him we may be united to God and to one another.'[2]

In one of those Easter Sunday evening sermons in Lincoln Cathedral:

> Easter Day is for us the central truth of our faith. But while we accept this far-reaching reference of Easter Day to the past and the future, is there not a danger lest we forget its meaning for us *now* in the present? The Resurrection of Christ has placed us *now* in a new sphere, in a new life, and brought us into contact with new forces: the Resurrection of Christ is for us a new power.[3]

And again on one such Easter evening in the cathedral:

> The greatness of our Easter Festival is not so much to be seen in the wonderful events which immediately attended it, as in the wonderful abiding results which followed after it, and from it . . . The reality and the greatness of Easter joy is to be found for us in the reality of the relation of the Resurrection of Christ to our own lives.[4]

Theologians delight to speak of realized eschatology, that is to say the sense we rightly have of those things which belong to the end and consummation of everything in history, already being experienced—albeit as in the words of Paul, 'only dimly as in a mirror'. Somewhat like the overture to an opera, we are given us a foretaste of what is to come later, to what John Robinson calls 'the end in the middle'.

Such is the event of the Transfiguration of Christ, so central to all three of the Synoptic Gospels, but which some biblical scholars used to excuse as being 'a misplaced resurrection appearance' — as though it had no right to be there, and yet, in exactly where it would seem, the gospel writers deliberately placed it. For it was precisely in that location and at that time in their journey of discipleship that we are told of the three sleepy disciples awakening to see Christ's glory (Luke 9:32)—the finished product to which Christ points paradoxically from the Cross: 'It is finished: It is accomplished' and, even now both in time, as well as beyond time.

And what is that glory defined as constituting? In the words of Irenaeus: 'The glory of God is a human being fully alive' —mature humanity, fully alive, measured by the stature of nothing less than the fullness of the glorified Christ.

RESURRECTION HOPE
FOR A GLORY TO BE REVEALED

King is sometimes criticized as being over optimistic at a time when the confident later Victorian culture believed in the natural progress of mankind. One is tempted to ask what would have been his response to the horrors of the First World War, to say nothing of the Holocaust and genocides of later years? A bland optimism would not have survived, as indeed from the evidence of recent years, it clearly has not. But King's outlook was not based on a bland optimism, but rather on the theological virtue of hope, itself, more fundamentally based on the contradiction of the Paschal Mystery and the victory of Easter Day overriding and reversing the apparent defeat and devastation of that previous Friday, which para- doxically and with hindsight, is persistently and paradoxically named as *Good* Friday. Christians and particularly an apostolic Church in the words of Roger Schultz, the founding prior of Taizé, should be known as a 'Resurrection People' with 'Alleluia as our song', specifically called to be witnesses of these things, and as contemporary 'Signs of Contradiction'—the seeming contradiction of the Paschal Mystery.

So King, working out the implications of the Resurrection of Christ in the lives of his followers, continues:

> 'Christ will finish this work *in* us, which he has finished *for* us, so as to present us whole without spot to the Father.' . . . We may then, *here in this life*, have the Spirit of Christ and walk in the Spirit. This is not to be regarded as a rare privilege belonging to a few great saints, but is a necessary condition of the Christian life.[5]

As such, what we might term the 'spiritual life' or 'Christian spirituality'.

'St Paul, in his Epistle to the Corinthians', says King in another of his Easter sermons, 'has given us evidence for the Resurrection of Christ regarded as a simple fact' in the past. 'And yet we find, some five years later, the great Apostle, in his Epistle to the Philippians, still praying that he might know Christ "and the power of his Resurrection".'

It was not enough for the great Apostle to accept the mere fact; it was the results of the fact, the full power of the Resurrection which the Apostle was still striving to know, and not only intellectually, but from *experience*, a key word with King, as we shall see: 'To know Him and the power of his Resurrection'.

King continues:

> So, brethren, it should be with us. We should not be satisfied with a mere intellectual assent to the evidences which convince our minds of

the fact of the Resurrection, but year by year,
as the great Festival comes round, we should
ask ourselves if we are growing in grace, and in
the knowledge of our Lord and Saviour, Jesus
Christ and of the power of his Resurrection,
and of the results which follow from it.[6]

There is a further consideration which follows from
this, which, King insists, 'is the most important of
all': 'I mean the result of the Resurrection upon our
own lives: "Therefore," says St Paul "we are buried
with Christ by baptism into death: that like as Christ
was raised from the dead by the glory of the Father,
even so we also should walk in *newness of life*."'[7]

'To St Paul, beyond the simple miraculous fact
of the Resurrection, if it was to be anything to him,
it must be an outflowing of an endless stream of
new life. Apostle as he was, it was the power of the
Risen life that he prayed he might know',[8] but with
a knowledge born of experience and not simply
derived, secondhand from mediated information.

THE GIFT OF NEW LIFE

King consistently spells out the nature of this transformation to new life and participation in the Paschal
Mystery which we celebrate at Easter.

Our joy is in newness of life. It is not merely the
change from an old to a new commandment,
but it is the gift of a new life. A new life implies
new powers; a new heart, a new mind, new
powers to renew our will. The new life implies

a new object, a new aim, a new end to our
living. Our new life comes from the risen and
ascended Saviour . . . The new powers which
we have received from the risen and ascended
Saviour make it possible *now* for us to set our
affections, our minds, on things above, not on
things on the earth. Newness of life implies not
only that we ought to do this but that we have
the power to do it, and not only that we have
received new power to do it as in obedience to
an external law, but that our very heart's desire
is changed and made new, so that the things
which we naturally despised, we value, and the
things which we naturally hated, we love, and
hate the things which we naturally desired.[9]

King is insistent and repeatedly so in other Easter
sermons that we have, that the spiritual life or that
new life of *the new humanity* is essentially nothing less
than a participation in the new risen life of Christ
himself:

Easter day not only tells us of our pardon
[through Christ's death], but also of a new state;
Christ has not only obtained for us pardon, but
He has also given us power, a new life: 'Because
I live,' says Christ, 'you shall live also'—the life
of the new humanity has had a new beginning
offered to it.[10]

For so many Christians throughout history, of all
traditions (with the possible exception of Eastern
Orthodoxy), such words could suggest that there
has been an over-emphasis on our pardon and justification obtained through the death of Christ, by
'stopping short' (in King's recurring turn of phrase)

with Ash Wednesday, Lent and Good Friday and yet, failing to follow through to celebrate and appropriate what Christ has done in us, as well as for us, in his Ascension, Glorification and the outpouring of his Holy Spirit. Thereby there has been a failure to run the full course of all that is implied by the Paschal Mystery.

> Therefore let us leave the elementary doctrine of Christ and go on to maturity, not laying again a foundation of repentance from dead works and of faith toward God, with instruction about ablutions, the laying on of hands, the resurrection of the dead and eternal judgement (Hebrews 6:1–5).

When speaking of those who 'leave the elementary' teaching and 'go on to maturity' the Epistle makes it clear a verse later, that they are 'those who have once been enlightened, who have tasted the heavenly gift, and have become partakers of the Holy Spirit, and have tasted the goodness of the word of God and the powers of the age to come'. That is the what 'running the full course' of discipleship is all about; that is the complete 'prescription' for that fullness of life, and for all that is implicit in the Paschal Mystery as well as constituting the vision that King both taught and exemplified as being the calling of all 'Christ-like Christians'.

So, King in no way short cuts or underplays the price of our redemption. On the contrary:

> We see our pardon comes from above, not from below; it comes from God to us, it comes down

from heaven to earth, its origin is in God, not in us . . . Our pardon came to us before we came to Him; 'We love because he first loved us . . . Our pardon originated in the infinite love of God . . . when we look back we are to see and remember that the pardon is complete . . . The debt of sin is paid off, the debt of the sins of the whole world, the handwriting which was against us, the whole bond which the enemy held for our conviction has been plucked out of his hand . . . The atonement—the at-one-ment, i.e., between God and man has been accomplished, God and sinners have been reconciled; reconciled back again into the relation which God intended man originally to have.[11]

While King would urge us to remember with thanksgiving the price of our redemption, he would not want us to get stuck with this, or 'stop short', but rather to press on and lay claim to our full inheritance as the children of God, and always, as his Easter sermons make abundantly clear, from all that Christ has gone on to do for us and in us by his Resurrection, Ascension, Glorification and the outpouring of His Holy Spirit. King repeats and reinforces this in a later Easter sermon:

It is not enough that we should be trying to be good in our own strength without the help of God; it is not enough that we should admire the moral excellence and beauty of the character and life of Christ. It is not enough that we should look back to the great scene on Calvary, where Christ offered up Himself as the one sufficient sacrifice, oblation and satisfaction for the sins of the whole world. We need to pass on from

41

Good Friday to Easter Day, and then not to rest merely in the acknowledgement of the fact of the Resurrection, but to know its *power*. This was Paul's idea of a true knowledge of Christ: 'That I might know Him, and the power of His Resurrection'.[12]

St Paul's desire to know 'the power of the resurrection' was not restricted simply to a belief in life after death, in the hereafter, but as King is adamant to affirm, the victory of Easter day holds good for 'the power of a new life *now*':

Christ has not only obtained our pardon and given us hopes of fuller glory, but he has made it possible for us to be in a state of grace *now*. Easter Day tells us of the victory over sin and the power for a new life *now*. We are, as Christians, in a state of grace, and we may live, and we ought to live spiritual lives.[13]

Yet, King is determined to go further still in reclaiming the fullness of our inheritance as the children of God achieved by the victory of Easter. While the willingness of Christ to lay down his life for others, as supremely exemplified in the taking up of his Cross is an example of the Christ-like life which Christian disciples should seek to emulate in every way, nevertheless such an 'exemplary theory of the atonement' (as it is often theologically spoken of), is here again, not sufficient: King would exhort us not to stop short but to lay hold on the source of that new, abundant life, by being nothing less than 'partakers' as well as sharing in the divine life of Christ himself.

> If our Easter joy is based on the revealed will of God in Holy Scripture, then the relation of the risen and ascended Christ to us will not be merely that of an external example, *but a new source of life* . . . If we are to rule our lives by faith in Christ, we must not only look up to Christ as the pattern of our lives, but we must look to Him as the source of *new life* and *power* by which that pattern may be followed. This is the joy of our Easter communion, because that in it we become partakers of Christ. He dwells in us, and we in Him.[14]

Here, King is precisely and deliberately echoing that phrase in the Prayer of Humble Access in Cranmer's Book of Common Prayer, when at Communion, we pray 'that we may evermore dwell in Him, and He in us'.

So far from such a claim or aspiration being the eclectic boast of monks and nuns, as being the spiritually privileged of the extra saintly few, King would assert such a claim as being the norm for all who have been baptized into Christ as members of the Church as the Mystical Body, resourced from scripture, the sacraments of the Church, worship and corporate as well as personal prayer.

'This is the knowledge of Him', King concludes, which St Paul continues to pray for' and as Christians, so must we, in every age. 'This is the power of His Resurrection which faith tells us may be ours today, and in which we may hope to overcome the world.'[15]

THE HOLY SPIRIT AND EXPERIENCE

On one of the several occasions outlined in the previous chapter when King listed the various constituent elements that give balance and harmony to any inner life of the Spirit, he demonstrated in that prescription for a healthy life in the Spirit, how all the seven elements are all inextricably bound together and are related to each other. At the same time, he freely admitted that the suggested order in which each flows on to another was not set in stone and that the order in which he had listed them will vary: for example, as said before, some will start on the journey of faith with a heightened sense of 'duty' and responsibility, driven and strongly motivated for social action and social justice, in what might loosely be termed public-school religion. Others may start from the opposite end of King's suggested list with some deep experience and awareness of God's love through the impact of the Holy Spirit in some kind of spiritual awakening.

Whenever or wherever on the spiritual pilgrimage of the heart any such experience of 'awakening' in whatever way we may speak of it or experience it, King consistently urges that we must not 'stop short', but must press on and follow through on our journey of faith. If we are to grow in the life of the Spirit, there must be no standing still, supposing that we 'have arrived'; neither must there be any turning back seeking to recapture a previous, possibly precious experience of a closer intimacy, or a 'consolation' as it is sometimes termed. Rather, there should always be a prevailing sense from start to finish that the best is yet to come, and therefore not to settle for second best or even for that which is quite good.

It was when speaking of two of those constituent elements—the Holy Spirit and the Church, that King cautions 'against thinking that we are living in the Spirit unless we are willing to be guided by the Church'.[16] On the face of it, such a claim might well smack of that arrogant control and power seeking of which the Church throughout the ages has been so insidiously conspicuous: seeking to control the freedom of the Spirit.

However, there is no Church that can claim to be the Church of Christ which is not that Spirit-filled body of which St Paul speaks so persistently throughout all his writings. The analogy of a 'body' as in I Corinthians, chapter 12, needs both structure and flexibility, form and spontaneity. In Ezekiel's valley of the dead bones, the bones and structure without the breath do not constitute a fully alive body, while contrary-wise, the breath without a container simply evaporates. Structure and form without spontaneity degenerate into a rigid formalism and yet the opposite—namely spontaneity without structure—will not do the trick either. The freedom of the dance for the human body still requires the structure of bones and muscle: a jelly fish can't dance precisely because it has no inner structure: each is interdependent, and similarly with the Church and the Holy Spirit. The Church is there to give visible and tangible expression to the invisible life of the Spirit as at Pentecost, so that each and every nation and culture can hear the universal message of the Gospel 'in their own language'.

In the course of King's Second Address, for the Quiet Day at the beginning of the 1897 Lambeth Conference, he makes a passing reference to 'the operation of the Holy Spirit':

> The Acts of the Apostles as the starting point of Church history, has been called 'The Gospel of the Holy Spirit', and it has been so called from the desire to trace the operation of the Holy Spirit in the Church, and to see its growth as the Body of Christ, deriving its life from Him, the living, ever-present ruling, guiding Head.[17]

However, if we are looking for a fully developed doctrine of the working of the Holy Spirit in such as we have of King's writings, we will look in vain. Yet, it most certainly does not follow that the workings of the Holy Spirit were not integral to King's experience of the indwelling Christ.

King begins his opening address after the earlier Eucharistic homily, with what he terms an apology — an apology for what had dogged him from the moment he accepted the professorship in Oxford. Several notable figures, including no less a scholarly and formidable prelate than Bishop Tait at the time, had pointed out that a man such as King, with only a pass degree to his name, rather than an honours degree, failed to constitute the stuff of which Oxford professors were expected to be made.

So here, at the very outset of his three addresses, King addresses this whole issue:

> One special difficulty besets me on this great and very rare occasion and that is that, very much of the little that I know was learnt from books which you yourselves have written, or is the result of turns of mind which you yourselves have given me by your conversation, so that the only source of knowledge from which I can hope to draw anything that I do not know that you have already known, is the source of my own experience. This is indeed very simple and humble compared with your own, but to me, at least, it is real; and, if one speaks at all, one must speak with a sense of message. Forgive me, then, if I should speak with too much earnestness, or seeming presumption, about things which are to you simple and obvious; to me, at least, they have been, and are, real.[18]

Some of that might quite reasonably be construed as speaking somewhat 'tongue in cheek', since King was no mean scholar, indeed possibly far more knowledgeable of ascetic, moral and pastoral theology than many of the bishops present on that occasion. Nevertheless, reading between the lines, King uses two words which carried a greater significance at that time than they would today: 'experience' and 'enthusiasm'.

Both words were central to the vocabulary of Wesley and the Evangelical Revival of the previous century. For centuries, and not least in the writings of Hooker, the 'three legged stool' as it was termed— tradition, scripture and reason—had constituted the process for formulating theology. Wesley, whom throughout this whole study we shall discover to be of such vast importance to King, added a fourth, namely that of 'experience'. Furthermore, that second word in King's address—'enthusiasm'—was likewise somewhat loaded and suspect, as being associated unacceptably with the evangelical and spiritual awakenings of Wesley and others.

The High and Dry churchmanship with which King was raised with his family in his early years, would have been somewhat suspicious of claiming any personal, let alone dramatic, experience of the Holy Spirit such as Wesley claimed, and would be equally cautious about enthusiasm in communicating the Gospel.

Bishop's Butler's response to John Wesley in one of their three recorded meetings, notably sums up the cautious attitude of most churchmen in King's day, to anything verging on 'enthusiasm' or direct 'experience' of the Holy Spirit: 'Sir,' Butler is recorded as having retorted, 'the pretending to extraordinary revelations and gifts of the Holy Ghost is a horrid thing, a very horrid thing.' Although Keble and the Puseyites generally would not have been so dismissive as Butler, nevertheless, with their characteristic, 'reserve', as it was termed, they would have been cautious about using such terminology with reference to the workings and gifts of the Holy Spirit, with what is referred to as 'a reserve in the communication of Christian knowledge'. The leaders of the Oxford Movement were all sufficiently affiliated with the established upper socio-economic groups of the time so that the attitudes and emotionalism associated with the piety of at least many of the Evangelicals were regarded with grave suspicion. While the Oxford Movement leaders could certainly be emotionally demonstrative in their personal lives and make use of strong sentiment and feeling in poetry, prayers and homiletic appeals, they were cautious about the role of excitement or overt passion in religious practice and especially as a basis for a way of demonstrating religious conviction.[19]

Not surprisingly, such caution however meant that the High and Dry churchmen throughout the eighteenth century found themselves in a double bind: not only were they suspicious of the emotionalism of Wesley and the Evangelical revival of the previous century, 'they were also distrustful of the rationalism, which they regarded as a corrosive force in contemporary religion'.[20]

Such a double bind meant that the established Church had failed to capture the ear of the culture throughout the eighteenth century. Yet, it would seem that King could hold this double bind together by employing in a creative tension, both heart and mind, reason as well as experience, or, in more modern terminology, both hemispheres of the brain—each infusing the other. In theological terminology we speak of this as the work, the operation or the communion of the Holy Spirit, experienced in the outpouring of the gifts as well as the fruits of the Spirit, both of which, it would seem, King had in spades.

A Love Surpassing Knowledge

A SPIRITUAL AWAKENING

It is precisely those very gifts and fruits of the Spirit
so evident in King's person and ministry, and the
distinctive difference they make in authenticating
both the claims of the gospel message, as well as the
integrity of its messengers, that would lead us to set
aside the lack of explicit references to the Holy Spirit
as such, in what we have of King's recorded words
and writings. More important, are the accompanying
workings and presence of, rather than the verbal
references to the Holy Spirit and the difference the
Holy Spirit makes in the life of the Church and of
Christian disciples, as in the words of Ignatius of
Latakia below, that were all too evidently clear in
King's person and presence to all who encountered
him.

> Without the Holy Spirit, God is far away,
> Christ stays in the past, the gospel is simply
> another organization, authority is a matter
> of propaganda, the liturgy is no more than
> an evolution, and Christian living is a slave
> mentality.
>
> Bᴜᴛ, in the Holy Spirit, the cosmos is resur-
> rected and groans with the birth pangs of the
> Kingdom, the risen Christ is here, the Gospel
> is the power of life, the Church shows forth
> the Trinity, authority is liberating knowledge,
> mission is Pentecost, the liturgy is both renewal
> and anticipation, and human action is deified.[21]

In the light of that reference to the self-evident difference the gifts of the Holy Spirit make and from

what we know of both King's person and teaching, it is surely almost irrelevant to probe for further evidence of any particular occasion or occasions that would signify an 'awakening' or further fresh outpouring of the Gift of the Spirit as being experienced by King: 'by their fruits you shall know them' was the acid test employed by Jesus for any discernment of the Spirit.

However, it so happens that when King was principal of Cuddesdon, he invited John Keble, two years before his death, to preach the Festival sermon for the tenth anniversary of the founding of the College. On that occasion, Keble, whom King admired, and a copy of whose book, *The Christian Year*, was King's bedside book, spoke quite explicitly of the distinctive marks of the working of the Holy Spirit, significantly giving the title to his sermon—'Pentecostal Fear'. 'In that sermon he spoke of the gift of the Spirit as the source of all godliness and as the basis of all Christian ministry. The theme of the Christian way was one of divinization, so embedded in the spirituality of the Greek Fathers, and which was so very clearly central to Keble's own spirituality'—and certainly as this whole study will seek to affirm, also equally that of King, although not so clearly articulated theologically either in his writings, teaching or preaching. What is so striking is that for Keble, the 'new life', the gift and indwelling of the Spirit together with deification and the call to be 'partakers of the Divine life' are all interchangeable with no need for specific verbal differentiation:

Christ is come, not indeed in the Body, but by a nearer, far nearer Presence—by His Spirit: not only *with* them, but *within* them. In Him they now live a new life, which they have entirely from Him; a life which is both His and theirs; whereby they are so joined to Him as to be verily and indeed partakers of a Divine nature . . . Yes, my brethren, this and no less was the mysterious Pentecost privilege and glory of those on whom the Holy Spirit first came down: a glory so high and inconceivable, that the Holy Fathers did not hesitate to call it even Deification, and Christianity, which teaches and confers it, they called 'a deifying discipline.[22]

The only difference between Keble and King in their experience, is a difference of vocabulary and terminology. That 'nearer presence' not only 'with them' but 'within them', reflects exactly, only even more specifically, what King consistently spoke of as 'the indwelling Christ'—or, as he sometimes spoke of the Holy Spirit of Christ as intimately 'indwelling' the believer. As we shall consistently see throughout this whole study, it is the Person of Christ or Jesus or 'the Saviour', who is central to King's spirituality, as also is that divinization of which Keble goes on to speak, with the only difference being again, in the choice of vocabulary.

So, in the conclusion to that same sermon, Keble draws a picture of the contrast between the ministry of two different clergy—'one of whom believes in the reality of the gift of the Divine life' (i.e. the Holy Spirit) 'and the holiness that it both brings and demands, and the other who does not'.

> One man goes about his parish with the ever-present belief, that both he and everyone whom he meets, had the Holy Spirit within him — both he and they by Holy Baptism, he also, in a peculiar sense, by Holy Orders. Another, perhaps, no less earnest in work, is mainly taken up with natural and social differences. One goes into a church, thinks of Isaiah's vision, says to himself, 'here is the Lord, sitting on his throne, high and lifted up, and his glory filling the place: here are the angels, hither Christ coming in His sacraments'. To another, the place is nothing mysterious; he thinks only of edification and comfortable prayers.[23]

We need have no doubt which was John Keble's, or indeed Edward King's own understanding or experience.

So, in the light of all this and perhaps especially in the light of all this, it might still be worth asking or probing for any evidence that King experienced in the course of his life, some kind of spiritual awakening from any further indwelling of the Holy Spirit? After all, John Wesley, whom King admired so much for his doctrine of perfection, speaks in vivid detail of that 'strange warming of the heart' which he experienced on a particular day in a particular place, and to which he attributes not only 'the assurance of sins forgiven' but the further empowerment of his ministry, opening the way to sanctification or perfection in Wesley's terminology, or that divinization of which Keble spoke. There is a clue, but only a faint clue, which might suggest something along similar lines of what could be spoken of as a further 'awakening' gifted to King as a personal experience, but which that 'reserve' so characteristic of the Tractarians somewhat inhibited him from speaking or writing about.

A SIGNIFICANT DATE

On 3 February 1852, shortly after King had come down from Oxford, he had set out on a pilgrimage to the Holy Land. It appears to have been the first time he had set foot out of England. Homesickness, added to sea sickness when crossing the Channel, as well as a sense of loneliness, travelling alone, or at least for most of the time, taken altogether, certainly impacted him profoundly, as he recorded in the diary he kept of his travels.

> The feelings with which one leaves one's home to wander on the continent for any length of time cannot be understood but by those who have experienced them, and by those they will never be forgotten.[24]

And never to be forgotten indeed was either that date—3 February—or whatever occurred on that day for, when half a century later, on that selfsame 3 February 1897, as bishop, King wrote in his diary for that same date:

> Quite true, February 3rd, 1897, i.e. after having been preserved with such exceeding mercy and goodness for forty-five years, how thankful and trustful one ought to be.

Yet, as though that were not sufficient, only three years later and significantly for that same date, 3 February and even more poignantly against the same dated entry:

> Yes, this is true more and more, now I am seventy: February 3, 1900. *Deo Gratias.*

There is a further final entry yet, written in a tremulous hand, only a matter of a few weeks before he died:

> Yes, again, this is true more and more, now I'm eighty. February 3rd, 1910. Verily, his mercy endureth for ever. *Deo gratias.*[25]

So it would seem a fair question to ask, as to what exactly was the long lasting significance of that date, 3 February, so vividly recalled to the end of his long life? Do the diary entries possibly recall a significant turning point on King's spiritual journey, a deepened experience of the power and love of God in some spiritual awakening of what could equally well be termed a further outpouring of the Holy Spirit which occurred on that date, so vividly embedded in King's inner consciousness? Is that why 3 February, the day he started his journey and pilgrimage to the Holy Land, had such a special and lasting significance, always recalled, documented and remembered with thanksgiving to the end of his life? Is it reading too much into this, to attribute to that same day, 3 February 1852, something of a further spiritual awakening, or that 'warming of the heart', so fondly and frequently recalled by John Wesley? To hazard such an interpretation of that clearly cherished day and date might be an important factor in seeking to account for the outstanding spiritual gifts of the Spirit with which King was so evidently blessed.

Certainly, it is clear from one of King's *Spiritual Letters* that King saw the need for further stages in the developing spiritual journey of discipleship, of which the sacrament of Confirmation could be seen as some kind of marker. In a letter from Cuddesdon in 1865 to Charlie—a young lad from King's earlier days as a curate in Wheatley—and written in response to the questions the young man had raised concerning the need for a specific experience of what he terms 'conversion', King makes an interesting comment:

> As for conversion, don't let that bother you' as it would seem, from the young man's letter, it had. 'The fact is there are two sorts of conversion: (1) From a life of thoughtless sin to godliness. (2) In a life of godliness to a closer walk with God. The second we both practise, and need to practise every day.

Clearly, Charlie, by this time a student at Culham Teacher Training College, had been bothered about this, possibly from some fellow evangelical student, who had come to Christ in some evangelistic campaign. So, King adds:

> Do not be put out by this. You will see before too long that their view of one conversion once for all does not practically do. They will sin again, and need fresh conversion.[26]

The words, 'The second we need to practise every

day' reflect something of the words of the Prayer of Confirmation in the Book of Common Prayer, so very familiar to King in the course of his many Confirmations, which emphasize the need to 'daily increase in the Holy Spirit more and more'.

It would seem that for King, the gift of the Holy Spirit had been experienced more consciously as being that mystical indwelling of Christ, or diviniza-tion, which for King is a very Christ-centred spirit-uality, as likewise for Wesley. In that list of inter-woven elements outlined earlier, in a developed spirituality where people start with that kick-start of some quite dramatic and memorable experience, King would have urged, as he always did, with the other elements which he listed as the ingredients of a full life in the Spirit, the need not to 'stop short' (that recurring phrase) in the unfolding journey of discipleship, but rather, 'forgetting what lies behind' to press forward from one degree of glory to another, to that fullness of the stature of Christ, the goal of all our striving and the point and end of all religion.

3

The New Life in the Mystical Body of Christ

The Church is not merely a human institution and therefore morally helpful to the individual life; but as Christians we need to consider what being in Christ means.[1]

THE DIVINE NATURE OF THE CHURCH

For the founding fathers of the Oxford Movement, and not least for Keble, to whom King was devoted, the nature of the Church that 'Christ has appointed', its authority and its worship, was the persistent source of so much bitter controversy throughout the whole of King's life. Indeed, it was John Keble's Assize Sermon, preached in the University Church of St Mary the Virgin in Oxford on 14 July 1833, which reasserted the authority and the divine nature of the Church in the face of Parliament's proposal to suppress two Irish archbishoprics and eight Irish bishoprics, along similar lines and for similar reasons, as rotten boroughs had been suppressed only a year previously in the Reform Bill of 1832. In Keble's book, however reasonable such reform and reorganization of the Church in Ireland might be, Parliament was not the appropriate nor divinely appointed body to undertake such reforms.

Viewed retrospectively it is clear, as indeed Newman later claimed, that in the Assize Sermon, Keble unwittingly had lit the fuse for the whole subsequent Movement by reasserting the nature of the Church as the Divine Society, and not simply as a human institution or organization, but rather as a living organism—nothing less than the mystical Body of Christ. In a letter from Cuddesdon as early as 1868, when King was principal of Cuddesdon Theological College, King had written 'The Church holds its powers from our Blessed Lord, not from the Queen or Parliament, and no man can take them away'.[2]

As King reminded the assembled bishops at Lambeth in 1897:

> The Church is not merely a human society and therefore morally helpful to the individual life; but as Christians we need to consider what being in Christ means. To be in Christ does not merely mean being placed in a system which Christ established, or which depends upon Him, or which is formed on the basis of His acts and doctrine; but, rather, to be a baptized Christian implies a real union with a living body, the life of which is in Him—a real introduction into the midst of heavenly powers by virtue of union with Him; a real state in which we are related to Him as branches to a vine, although that relation may be forfeited by our unfaithfulness.[3]

THE APOSTOLIC SUCCESSION

With such a high view of the nature of the Church, however inept, immoral or ineffective the priests and bishops of the Church have been throughout the ages, nevertheless in so much of his writings and teaching, King consistently sought to recover the true nature of the priestly ministry as being primarily 'ministers or stewards' entrusted with 'the cure of souls', embodying in their persons a living tradition, faithfully handing on to others 'that which they first received', and not simply as managers of an organization. In the words of King: 'Organization does not produce life, though life may produce organization—but the secret of the power is the life.'[4]

The founding fathers of the Oxford Movement were adamant to a man in reasserting:

> The Church is not primarily a human institution. However lethargic and even corrupt the Church may appear, it is divine in origin and is the theatre for the drama of God's special acts of grace. The apostolic succession is a vital doctrine ensuring the continuity of divine purpose, and so the Church of England was not to be viewed as some part-Protestant and part-Catholic quasi-political entity produced in reformation conflict. It is more than a *via media.* It is a living extension of the ancient Church. It is God's Church.[5]

DISESTABLISHMENT

Throughout the whole of King's life the question of the disestablishment of the Church of England was always in the sub-text of various proposals: Newman still hoped for a 'Churched-England' while Keble recognized that the separation of disestablishment was likely to be the only answer. King, as usual, was not over perturbed either way.

> The Church has many enemies just now, and infidelity is making itself felt in high places, but I see no reason in that to fear; indeed, I rejoice because I believe it will make people think and look a bit deeper into things . . . All these anxieties about the Establishment need not trouble you . . . the Church existed for 300 years without being joined to the State, and could just as well exist again.[6]

King along with the Tractarians of the Oxford Movement never doubted in his own mind that the Church of England, albeit by law established, was nevertheless a true and unbroken continuation of the Church of the apostles, bearing the three classic marks of Holiness, Catholicity and Apostolicity, while lamenting its disunity in its present, earthly form. Unlike Newman and others of the early fathers of the Oxford Movement, it would seem that King was never attracted or deflected by the aggressive claims of Rome, which asserted not only that the Elizabethan settlement had rendered the Church of England no longer a part of the one true Church, but also, and in particular in the papal bull, *Apostolicae Curae*, of 1896, that the apostolic line had been broken at the Reformation, rendering Anglican orders invalid.

King, in keeping with the teaching of the Oxford Movement, and in the tradition of the Caroline Divines of an earlier century recovered what we would wish to term a 'high doctrine' of the Church. The Risen and Ascended Saviour in the new covenant is 'the Bridegroom of the Church, He is the Head of the Church, He knows her needs, He can give her new power from the inexhaustible fountain of his own divine life: as He lives by the Father, so the Church draws her life from Him'.[7]

> There is a society called the Church, claiming to be the covenanted sphere of the Divine love; not the *exclusive* sphere, not hindering God from working elsewhere, but having the promise that we shall find him *there* — 'The place that He had chosen to put His Name there'.[8]

THE HOLY SPIRIT AND THE CHURCH OF GOD

In claiming any authority for the Church, its ministry, its sacraments or scriptures, King always resorts to one single source for that authority, namely the Person of Christ to whom all authority had been given in the first place, subsequently bequeathed after his Ascension and Glorification in the gift of the Holy Spirit to continue Christ's real and affective presence in the world 'at all times and in all places' for the empowerment of the Church and its ministry.

King's apparent lack of explicit references to the work and gift of the Holy Spirit, as in the previous chapter is perfectly understandable for there is a sense in which we cannot 'know' the Holy Spirit, by way of a personal relationship in quite the same way as we can 'know' the person of the Jesus of history or the Christ of faith. Rather, all we can see, are the effects of its presence and workings, in a similar fashion to how we can see and hear the wind bending the branches of trees or the crashing waves of a storm at sea. We experience its drawing power like the magnetic power between the two poles of a magnet which draws what it attracts into its magnetic field. Perhaps, similarly, we are drawn, as we say, into the 'fellowship'—*koinonia*—of the Holy Spirit into that field of love 'proceeding', as we say in the Creeds, from the Father and the Son. The magnetic power is not *in* either of the poles of the magnet, in a self-sufficient way, but rather it is in the magnetic field between the two, in what John Taylor, speaking of the Holy Spirit, calls the *go-between God*.[9]

Taylor suggests that 'in every encounter' like falling in love, or worship which 'makes a landscape or a person or an idea come to life', it is as though

> there has been an anonymous third party who makes the introduction, acts as a go-between, makes two beings aware of each other, sets up a current of communication between them . . . Christians find it quite natural to give a personal

name to this current of communication, this
invisible go-between. They call him the Holy
Spirit, the Spirit of God ... That is the Spirit
which Christ promised to send to his friends
and on the day of Pentecost, that is the Spirit
which came and possessed them just as he had
possessed Jesus.[10]

That field of fellowship is the Church as a continuing extension of the Incarnation, experienced as
the mystical Body of Christ, formed by the 'overshadowing' — *episkiazo* — of the Holy Spirit as also in
the *epiclesis*, or 'calling down' of Holy Spirit in the
Eucharist to form the Blessed Sacrament as the Body
of Christ. Furthermore, it is in that same 'overshadowing' of the Holy Spirit of Mary, whereby the body
of the Christ child was formed within her, according
to Luke's account of the Annunciation (Luke 1:35). It
is in that sense, that we rightly speak of the first Pentecost as being the birthday of the Christian Church.

There are some theologians, mainly of the Orthodox Churches of the East who claim that the Feast
of the Transfiguration marks the conception of the
Church, as the three bewildered disciples in that
account enter the cloud and are 'overshadowed' —
that same word *episkiazo* — by the Holy Spirit (Luke
9:34).

What is abundantly clear in all of this, is that the
fellowship of the Church is drawn together and
made visible in time and space by the Holy Spirit.
Similarly, and possibly even more mysteriously and
counterintuitively is that moment in one eucharistic

Anglican liturgy when the priest, quoting from the scriptures, turns to the gathered congregation and addresses them with the words, 'We are the Body of Christ, by the one Spirit we were all baptized into one Body' and all alike, from start to finish, perceived as the work of the Holy Spirit:

> The Holy Spirit is not only, so to say, engaged in working out our individual perfection, but He knows the part of the Body of Christ which we are wanted to supply, and He is preparing us for that. He knows the whole plan of the House of God, which is the Church of the living God.[11]

So, for King this new life with its attendant powers is lived out, most definitely not as individuals but as interdependent members of a living organism, the Church of God, discerned as nothing less, in true Pauline language, than the mystical Body of Christ, deriving both its authority and its spiritual power from God, formed and resourced by the 'overshadowing' and outpouring of the Holy Spirit, and furthermore, not simply as an organization to forward the teaching of the Christian life with its services of worship and good works in the community.

> In the Apostles' Creed . . . as it was recited in the third century, there was a slight difference, whereby the clause 'Holy Church' stood last of all at the end of the Creed, and sometimes with a word added — *through* — 'through the Holy Church'; thus declaring in express terms what elsewhere is always implied, that it is through, or by our being incorporated into the Church of Christ's Body, that we have the Communion of

Saints, remission of sins and the Resurrection of
the flesh and life everlasting. Thus the Church
is put before us as the covenanted system of
God's Love—as the sphere in which God has
provided that the new life of the risen and
ascended Saviour should come to each one
of us.[12]

So, it follows therefore, as King consistently claims:

The Christian Creed is not a system, but a life;
it implies a complete devotion of mind and
heart and of conscience and will to Christ. This
life and this liberty are based on supernatural
truth and power; it is this supernatural truth,
this truth revealed through Christ, which makes
us free from the guilt and bondage of sin. This
supernatural truth and power, this truth as it is
in Jesus, comes to us as Jesus has provided that it
should come, by the ministry of the sacraments
and the Word in His Church. It is as members
of his Body the Church that we enter into and
enjoy the full blessings of the glorious liberty
of the children of God; the righteousness of
Christ is our righteousness; because he lives
we live also; Christ in us is our hope of glory.[13]

So, by way of a wrap-up—'now you can understand', says King as the peroration one year to his
Easter proclamation, 'why it is that we are so anxious
that you should all be full members of the Church
of Christ, in the fullest possible way—because the
Father, having "put all things under His feet has
given Him to be the Head over all things to the
Church, which is His Body—the fullness of Him
that filleth all in all".' [14]

In King's ecclesiology, the Church exists for two main reasons, not only to teach and preach, but also by both Word and Sacrament, to empower all members of the Church to live the risen life of Christ, personally and corporately. 'The Church is the society which the Saviour founded to teach man God's perfect Will' and also 'to give him the means of grace which should enable him to do it'.[15]

THE SACRAMENTS OF THE CHURCH AND THE SACRAMENTAL PRINCIPLE

One of the classic definitions of a sacrament is something that is an outward and visible sign of an inward, invisible grace. In the Christian Church there are different rituals that are considered to be sacraments—Baptism, Confirmation. Communion, Matrimony, Ordination and the Anointing of the Sick—all of which have a physical, material sign which points beyond the outward expression to the greater significance of the Spirit, whether it be the bread and wine, the water of Baptism, the oil of Ordination and the Anointing of the Sick or the ring on the finger in the sacrament of Matrimony. All material symbols signify a deeper spiritual reality which always requires, as King insists, 'the aid of the Holy Spirit "Who searcheth all things, yea, the deep things of God". For as St Chrysostom says, "There is need of spiritual wisdom that we may perceive things spiritual".'[16]

The daily Eucharist had always featured as clearly central to King's spirituality and continued to be so to the end of his life. During the two years King had been 'squatting' at Hilton House, in Lincoln, prior to moving into the Old Palace, he had taken a portable little altar which had formally belonged to Pusey and used it for his daily celebration, while waiting for the work on the Old Palace to be completed.[17]

It's the sheer physicality of the Eucharist as with the sacrament of matrimony—'with my body I thee worship'—in which union in communion is sealed by inwardly ingesting material objects in the form of bread and wine, which, when discerned and indeed experienced by the 'wisdom' of the Spirit, carry a far greater significance as being nothing less than the Body and Blood of Christ.

'Man is what he eats.' With that statement, the German materialistic philosopher Feuerbach thought he had put an end to all "idealistic" speculations about human nature. 'On the contrary', asserts Schmemann, 'he was expressing, without knowing it, the most religious idea of man.'[18] So in the words of Augustine, 'We eat the Body of Christ, so as to become the Body of Christ'.

Yet the sacramental principle insists that our attention is not arrested by the outward form, but rather is drawn further to where it points and to what it signifies: here again, to use King's turn of phrase, we must not 'stop short' with what is visible on the surface, but go deeper to lay hold of the inward meaning, which is only revealed to the spiritually minded and with the eyes of faith.

THE AUTHORITY OF SCRIPTURE

In the same way as King had reasserted the authority of the Church with its sacraments, he was equally confident to reassert the authority of the Bible, as deriving its authority from the same source, namely, the person of Christ, the living Word to whom both the Church and the sacraments together with the scriptures point:

> His mind was steeped in the Bible; he believed fully in its inspiration; it was its inner meaning that he was continually dwelling upon. He took little interest in textual criticism, or historical criticism. He was hardly aware of the synoptic problems. His object in reading the Bible was to penetrate to the mind of his Lord and Saviour. His preaching and teaching was the very breath of the Scriptures . . . He made it, if possible, his daily duty to weigh well the Scriptures.[19]

Inevitably, in King's day, as in our own, there were those who felt that any word or words within scripture to which we applied the critical faculties of any other discipline—be it literary or historical—would result in the demolition of the whole edifice: such of several at the time, was one—John William Burgon (1813–88). Burgon had been King's tutor, during King's time as a student at Oriel. With his considera-

ble scholarship he defended the Mosaic authorship
of Genesis and biblical inerrancy in general.

> Either with the best and wisest of all ages,
> you must believe *the whole* of Holy Scripture;
> or, with the narrow minded infidel, you must
> *dis*believe the whole. There is no middle course
> open to you.[20]

King, who was devoted to and saturated in the scriptures, as all his printed sermons so clearly demonstrate, and who was never threatened by the new
learning in general or the encroachment of literary
or historical criticism with regard to the scriptures
in particular, nor indeed to anything or anyone else
genuinely seeking truth, pitches right in with those
addresses to the Lambeth bishops in 1897 on this
very topic. For the second address of that Quiet Day,
he took the text: 'You search the scriptures because
you think that in them you have eternal life: and
they are they which testify to me. And yet you will
not come to me that you might have eternal life'
(John 5:39):

> I cannot speak to you, my most reverend and
> right reverend brethren, of the highest criticism;
> it is for you to speak to me of that, but I wish
> to venture to call your attention to this text,
> in which the Saviour finds fault with those
> who apparently did spend a good deal of time
> over the Scriptures, with a certain amount of
> belief, and yet stopped short of what the Saviour
> wanted them to learn. They were inclined to
> rest in the letter of the Old Testament instead of
> interpreting it by the help of the Living Word;

they were inclined to *repose* where they should
have been moved to *expectation;* they set up
a theory of holy Scripture which was really
opposed to the Divine purpose of it: 'Ye search
the scriptures, and ye will not come to Me, that
ye might have life.'

It was Charles Marriott who used to say,
though as you know he was a true scholar,
and quite willing that scholarship and honest
criticism should have full freedom to do its
own work—he used to say: 'The utmost that
criticism can do is to prepare a correct text for
the reading of the Spiritual Eye.'[21]

Of course King was fully aware of the apparently
destructive scholarship with regards to the authority of scripture, but he did not go down the road
of biblical fundamentalism or literalism with the
likes of Burgon or others who shared that approach.
Rather, he cut the Gordian knot by suggesting an
alternative way, or in his words, 'a more real way of
reading our bibles' which transcends both biblical
criticism on the one hand, and scriptural literalism
or fundamentalism on the other:

Now what I am anxious to say is, that in the face
of these new forces, and in order that we may
direct them aright, some of us at least need to
make our way of reading the Bible more *real.*[22]

The remedy suggested for this danger as being a
more *real* way of reading the scriptures, recalls what
for many centuries was termed *lectio divina.* Such
a way of reading the scriptures, in King's words,
required 'a prayerful and patient waiting for the

unfolding of the meaning of the deeper texts, and this in order that we may first keep before ourselves, and our people, the true standard of Christian ethics'.

So in order to gain the right kind of 'knowledge' of God's revelation derived from the Bible, King insisted that it was necessary to read the scriptures (especially the Old Testament) from the perspective of the Jesus of the New Testament, allowing the written words to point the reader to the living Word, made explicit in the person of Christ, as in the story of the Road to Emmaus: 'Beginning with Moses and all the prophets, he interpreted to them in all the scriptures the things concerning himself' (Luke 24:27).

Here again as with everything else, for King it was always the same and a matter of 'not stopping short' and getting stuck in the letter of the text, albeit a text corrected, as far as possible, by the best literary criticism. Rather, he urges the need to go further and to read the written word with the 'spiritual eye' or 'inner eye' which points beyond the literal text to the Word made flesh, the living Word—the person of Christ.

So again, King continues:

> My learned and saintly predecessor, Bishop Christopher Wordsworth, wrote, as you know, a Commentary on the whole Bible. It is obvious that any person undertaking such a task as that could not be expected to do full justice to each single word; but I would venture to submit that if anyone would read consecutively the Prolegomena to the different books of the Bible

in Bishop Wordsworth's Commentary, he would get a most valuable insight into the spiritual connection and articulation and scope of the whole revelation of God's will, so as to feel that he was following the Saviour's own method of teaching the old Scriptures . . . Christ is really the key to the Old Testament; there are things written in the Law of Moses, and in the prophets, and in the Psalms concerning *Him* — the Law is our schoolmaster to bring us unto Christ.[23]

The danger against which the Saviour warns us in the text is the danger of not coming to Him as the source of our new life. We may stop short even in a wrong study of the Scriptures as well as in other ways.[24]

Such a method of reading the scriptures in the way that King urged was totally in keeping with both the spirit of the age as well as the Tractarians:

Influences from the contemporary Romanticism in combination with the study of the Fathers, not least those of the Alexandrian school, led the Tractarians not only to 'a symbolic or sacramental view of nature, according to which the visible world can be regarded as an index or token of the invisible', but also to a sacramental view of the Scriptures. 'Every word of Revelation has a deep meaning,' says Newman in his *Lectures on the Prophetical Office of the Church*. 'It is the outward form of heavenly truth, and in this sense a mystery or a Sacrament.'[25]

Furthermore, and perhaps of greater significance, is the fact that King's approach to reading the scriptures was also in line with, and indeed possibly directly influenced by, his friend Keble, with his approach to reading not only scripture, but all literature and especially poetry, as for a time professor of poetry at Oxford.

> Keble knew well the inadequacy of human language to convey the mystery of God. He was suspicious of the easy religion of slogans and of the equally easy religion of superficially stirred endeavours, both of which he saw as characteristic of much of the popular Evangelicalism of his day. He was no less critical of a rationalistic theology in which moral truth became a matter of syllogism. Faith was indeed of the heart as well as of the head, but it was not of a heart worn upon the sleeve.[26]

In his tract, *On the Mysticism Attributed to the Early Fathers of the Church*, which appeared in 1839, Keble wrote:

> Consider how very differently the same words sound in our ears, according to our different moods of mind; how much more meaning we find, not only in the text of scripture, but in a chance passage of a book or a stray remark of a friend, when we recall it by and by, more seriously than at first we listened to it; nay, and how much beyond what we suspected we discover occasionally in our own words, uttered perhaps at first by instinct, we hardly knew how; so that not only are we always uncertain whether any two persons receive exactly the same impression—the same moral impression, that is—from any given words, but even, whether to the same person the same ideas are conveyed by them twice. And yet there is truth and definite meaning in the words so

spoken although they go so much deeper with one man than they do with another.[27]

WORSHIP AND RITUAL

King's whole approach to reading scripture in a quasi-sacramental way, as indicated above, and by not stopping short but going deeper to uncover the inner significance of the words, holds good in every aspect of his theology and ecclesiology. Although King undoubtedly had what we would term a 'high doctrine' of the Church, as well as of scripture, he nevertheless saw the need to hold any zeal or love for the Church in check.

> It is needful to caution some to beware of trusting to their zeal for the Church, unless they really look to Christ—the example of His life, the reality of forgiveness through the atoning virtue of His death, and the power of his resurrection.[28]

So for King, the Church, in both its lifestyle and its worship, like the scriptures and the sacraments, must point beyond itself to the person of Christ and his Kingdom: it is a covenanted means of grace and not an end in itself. Although accused falsely of being a ritualist, he perceived with every bone in his body the dangers of ritualism which, like literalism with regard to reading the scriptures, can so easily become an end in itself. The Church, like everything in creation, is intended to be an icon, pointing beyond itself, rather than an idol, which seeks to draw attention to itself—as being an end in itself, rather than as a means to a greater end.

As the history of icons makes only too clear, the overlay of jewelry and cosmetic decoration on icons leads to their corruption as being objects of worship in themselves, which in turn inevitably and subsequently invites a time of iconoclastic reaction in which, sadly, both the outward form which has deteriorated into formalism, together with the inner substance, are both alike, as proverbially with the baby and the bath water, thrown out—at least for a season.

King continues to apply the same formula of not stopping short to the vexed question of ritualism:

> It is obvious, for example, that we may stop short in the wrong use of ritual . . . Bishop Butler in his Charge to the clergy of Durham in 1751 [says] . . . 'The form of religion may indeed be where there is little of the thing itself, but the thing itself cannot be preserved amongst mankind without the form.' Unless we bear this in mind, unless we make the externals of religion more and more subservient to promote the reality and power of it, we may be like the Jews who searched the Scriptures but would not come to Christ that they might have life; the mere external enjoyment of ritual is, in truth, only a modern form of Epicureanism, in fact materialism, and has no attraction for the really spiritually minded among our people, and no true power of spiritual edification.[29]

UNION, COMMUNION AND
THE UNITY OF THE CHURCH

In all these matters, whether a question of the authority of the Church as the Mystical Body of Christ,
the authority of the ministry, the sacraments and
scripture or the place of ritual in worship—to all
alike, King applies the same formula of not 'stopping
short', but rather of pressing on to where all these
and other elements listed by King should point. All
alike are intended to point to the person of Christ
in whom alone is that true unity for which Christ
himself prayed, so that 'they may all be one'.

But such a unity is essentially a union and communion before it is a visible organizational unity.
For the danger in King's day as not least in our own
day, in these as in other matters, is the temptation to
abstract ecumenism as an end in itself, rather than
perceiving it as a byproduct of something much
deeper.

In the pursuit of ecumenism, King, in so many
ways, was ahead of his time: the age of ecumenism
didn't really get under way until after his death.
The mid-twentieth century marked the beginning
of various 'schemes' which sought to join differing
bodies of Christian Churches together in a kind of
ecclesiastical joinery seeking to reach something of
a compromise in matters of doctrine and dogma.
King, in this, as in other matters sought to go deeper
insisting that by being closer, like spokes in the hub
of a wheel at the centre, where, when re-centred in

Christ, we would indeed all be one in Christ as He is one with His Father and ours in the unity and communion of the Holy Spirit. As King pointed out in a letter to the Methodist Conference meeting in Lincoln in 1909. By being more 'Christ-like Christians, the more they would be like Christ and the nearer they would get to one another, and thus realize the Saviour's prayer that they all might be one'.

Indeed from King's perspective, it was the Established Church's lack of spiritual depth which he viewed as being the principal cause of the Methodist break away:

> I always felt that it was the want of spiritual life in the Church and brotherly love which led [the Methodists] to separate. The more we can draw near to Christ ourselves and fill ourselves with His Spirit, the greater power we shall have for unity.[30]

Drawing nearer to Christ, and a lively participating in the fellowship and communion of the Holy Spirit represent the lasting significance not only of King's own life and ministry as being the core of his own spirituality, but the goal of all our seeking and striving, both individually as well as corporately.

4

The World as Sacrament

All nature was to him a burning bush aflame with God.[1]

KING'S LOVE OF NATURE

Throughout his life, King had what might be described as an almost Franciscan joy in nature, with his love of birds and trees and plants and flowers. A little over four years or so before he died, as an old man of seventy-six, he preached a great sermon of thanksgiving in Lincoln Cathedral to mark the end of the typhoid epidemic, culminating in what might be conceived of as being almost a personal *benedicite omnia opera*:

> I will thank God for the pleasures given me through my senses, for the glory of the thunder, for the mystery of music, the singing of birds and the laughter of children. I will thank him for the pleasures of seeing, for the delights through colour, for the awe of the sunset, for the beauty of flowers, the smile of friendship and the look of love; for the changing beauty of the clouds, for the wild roses in the hedges, for the form and beauty of birds, for the leaves on the trees

through the winter, teaching us that death is sleep and not destruction, for the sweetness of flowers and the scent of hay. Truly, O Lord, the earth is full of thy riches.[2]

As the second son of a country parson, brought up in Stone parish in the county of Kent; trained as a curate also in the country parish of Wheatley outside Oxford; later, serving as the vicar of Cuddesdon and principal of the Theological College and finally, for twenty-five years as bishop of the far-flung rural and agricultural diocese of Lincoln, King, throughout his life, retained a deep love of nature and was never more at home than when walking or, as in his early years, riding through the countryside.

One of his early biographers writes:

> All the sights and sounds of Nature were dear to him. As a boy he had loved birds-nesting, bird-stuffing, and egg-collecting, and to the end of his life the habits of birds were full of interest to him. It was the same with flowers. Whenever he arrived in a fresh place, one of his first enquiries was about the local *flora*, and he would eagerly purchase any book bearing on the subject.[3]

A lady friend, and one of King's holiday companions with him in Switzerland, claims that 'one of the great pleasures of the holiday for the bishop was the flowers; he was a keen botanist, and lover of flowers, especially of the Alpine ones, and would draw your attention to their delicacy and fragility'. The world of nature and of creation, always spoke to King of the Creator and as being 'God's first text' and therefore as such, reflecting something of God's image. 'At Evolena when he was looking at a patch of saxifrage growing on a rock, he quoted from Dr Moberly's book, *Sorrow, Sin and Beauty*, and said it lay in us to be beautiful, far transcending the lily.'[4]

Natural history was frequently an interest and pursuit of the country clergy who often spent the larger part of their lives in the same parish, noting and observing the change of seasons, and the migration of birds; recording detailed accounts of local flora, butterflies and animals, as amateur botanists. So, from his earliest years, and undoubtedly strongly influenced by the rural setting and countryside of his father's parish in Kent, Edward King acquired an increasing love of the natural world. Although King never had a very deep knowledge of botany, an interest for which he had originally caught from his elder sister Anne, he loved plants and flowers. 'I still love birds and flowers,' he wrote towards the end of his life, 'the marvellous creation of a bird's nest.'[5] And again in those same last years at Lincoln, while still vigorously visiting his extensive countryside parishes: 'I still go on in my simple superficial way, loving flowers and birds, and the sunlight on the apples and the sunset, and like to think more and more of the verse, "With Thee is the well of life, and in Thy light shall we see light."'[6]

When he preached in rural parish churches, as he so frequently did during his twenty five years as bishop of Lincoln, he would draw his illustrations from the life of the country people, from the natural world of their environment all of which he knew first hand. There was nothing second hand or patronizing as he chose to speak in the language of those who were so deeply influenced by him.

Similarly, Jesus in the Gospel accounts of his ministry and teaching, varied his language and illustrations in accordance with the location in which he was ministering. In the south, in Jerusalem and the surrounding areas, the language is religious, the language of the religious establishment and the teachers of the law, while in the north and the countryside of Galilee with its lake and in the more rural areas, the illustrations are all drawn from nature—the lilies of the field and the birds of the air—or from the occupations of the local workforce, whether shepherds, farmers or fishermen. The language and illustrations varied, but the message was the same.

In his teaching and preaching, and especially in the course of his round of Confirmations each year, whether confirming farm hands, the village boys and girls or the agricultural workers, the bishop would speak their language using, as Christ himself did, analogies and the symbols of the natural world with an unselfconscious authenticity, neither forced nor condescending.

His chaplain throughout most of the Lincoln years, gives a particular example of how he used images from the natural world to drive home a deeper theological lesson or a story from the Bible.

In a Confirmation sermon during Epiphany-tide with the story of the Wise Men and the star, King does not start at the Bible end, so to speak, but rather chooses to connect first with an illustration which might capture the imagination of those—in this case some village lads—listening to him.

> Most boys collect something out of the wonders of Nature, either the eggs of birds, or butterflies, or flowers. Take care not to be cruel or wasteful of what is so beautiful and so wonderful, and then it is good to collect.

He has their attention, and has connected with what will resonate with their interests at that stage. But then, characteristically, he clearly wants to lead them further by urging them, in his well-tried formula, not to 'stop short', but to press on and go further and deeper:

> But don't stop at mere collecting; try and read about what you collect; try and learn something more of the laws and the life of the beautiful things which attract you, and you will be led on, if you follow right, as the Wise Men were by the Star, to see how all things are linked together in golden bands of wisdom and love; how all things come of Him, and should lead us to Him.[7]

This is but one illustration of the spiritual attentiveness and amazing awareness which inhabited King's whole person and not least in respect of the natural world around him. 'Alert and alive to all around him throughout his life, he felt in sympathy and harmony with nature, and in some strange way in league with the animals and beasts of the field, somewhat in the reputed spirit of St Francis'.[8]

And yet, King's sympathy would go much deeper than that. He had what might be defined as some kind of 'fine-tuning device' built into his make-up, which made him extraordinarily sensitive to the moods and feelings of others. Under the influence of the Bible, Wordsworth's poems and Keble's *Christian Year*, he had learned to discern a sacramental significance in nature, as God's creation.

THE ROMANTIC MOVEMENT
AND THE LAKE POETS

The age of King, of course, is that of the full flowering of the Romantic Movement, born from the works of the Lake poets of the previous century, in particular, Wordsworth and Coleridge, whose love of nature, in reaction against the urban and increasingly industrialized life of the city, is immortalized in their poetry.

> The idea that the contented life was the earth-connected life, even that goodness was embeddedness, had its roots in the 1790s, perhaps drawing on what Wordsworth and Coleridge had read of Rousseau . . . Co-presence with the natural world, a closeness that was inaccessible in what Coleridge always described as the 'dim' light of the city—the persistent coal smog of eighteenth century London—was somehow a release into a form of wellbeing which normal,

political, commercial, professional or even educational life would not only fail to approach but would actually disrupt and destroy. It is a powerful connection to make a love of nature as the route both to a love of truth and to a love of man'—which King would have loudly applauded and to which he would undoubtedly have added also, 'a love of God'.[9]

WORDSWORTH'S LOVE OF NATURE

One Christmas during his years at Lincoln, a friend had sent the bishop, as a Christmas present, some volumes of Wordsworth's poems. In a letter expressing his gratitude for the present, King wrote:

> It is a most beautiful and usable Wordsworth, and I am particularly glad to have it, as he seems to suit me. His love of all nature, and his constant use of it are a link to higher things which I greatly love; and his philosophical reflections, which some might think heavy, and others not purely metaphysical enough, just suit my capacities, so his poetry rests and refreshes me with new strength of head and heart, of thought and love.[10]

In his early life, Wordsworth had been deeply unhappy, packed off together with his sister Dorothy, after their mother's early death, to grandparents for their early upbringing. In adolescence, the young Wordsworth saw himself as something of a revolutionary radical with only a loose connection to the Christian faith, and with little time for the Established Church or the Establishment generally. Initially, and in the early days of the French Revolution, he was openly supportive of the early visionaries of the Revolution, although later and predictably, he reacted with deep disillusionment in the face of the later atrocities. It was precisely that disillusionment which led him to go deeper than the superficial outward appearance of the world around him and, in his case with specific reference to the world of Nature with which he had always had, from his earliest days, such a very close affinity.

In a sermon King refers to that inner spiritual journey of Wordsworth with regard to a deeper awareness of the natural world:

> Wordsworth speaks of his delight in Nature in the early days of his youth. 'Nature,' he says, 'was all in all to me. I had no need of any charm by thought supplied, or any interest unborrowed from the eye.'
>
> That was the beginning of his pleasure, but then Wordsworth adds, as he grows older, that time is past. 'For this do I not faint nor mourn, nor murmur, for I have learned to look on Nature, not as in the hour of thoughtless youth, but learning oftentimes the still sad music of humanity. And I have felt a presence that disturbs me with the joy of elevated thought, a sense sublime of something far more deep. Therefore am I still a lover of the meadows, and the woods and mountains — rather say love them with warmer love. Oh! With far deeper zeal of holier love.'

King then proceeds to seize on this to drive home a

sacramental world view which can love and revere the beauty of the natural world and yet, by not 'stopping short', can also press on to seek the hidden depths and significant meaning hidden beneath such outward forms of beauty, as indeed Wordsworth clearly did. In the particular case of Wordsworth it led to a deeper Christian faith: indeed, in his later years, he actually became a churchwarden in his local parish church.

So King seizes on the example of Wordsworth's inner journey of the spirit as the appropriate way to look at the beauty of created things in general:

> This is surely the true way of looking at the beauty of created things, and it has been exquisitely expressed by many of our own poets, by none, perhaps, with greater sweetness than by Wordsworth . . . This is surely what we need; not to shut our eyes to the beauties which God has entrusted to us; not to make the visible the end and aim of our happiness, but *through* the visible always to be led up to the thought of the invisible. This is the difference between the right and wrong loving of the world. We are right when the aim and governing principle of our life belongs to the Invisible, for then we are really looking not at the things that are seen, but at the things that are not seen.[11]

It is not surprising that King found the poetry of Wordsworth as something which 'seemed to suit' him, refreshing him 'with new strength of head and heart, of thought and love' because of the new way in which Wordsworth, through his poetry, as Keats put it, sought to 'think into the human heart',[12] thereby storming the powerful citadel of rationalism which had dominated the world of letters in the eighteenth century. Likewise, the unhappy and tortured agnostic, Frederick William Henry Myers, in his biography of Wordsworth, claimed that Wordsworth should be 'venerated because he has shown by the subtle intensity of his own emotion how the contemplation of Nature can be made a revealing agency, like Love or Prayer—an opening, if indeed there be any opening, into the transcendent world'.[13]

KEBLE

King also had a similar high regard for the poetry of John Keble, in particular for Keble's poems in *The Christian Year*, which was a lifetime's bedside companion, and from which King frequently quoted in his sermons and teaching. *The Christian Year* was published in 1827 and proved to be massively popular, being reproduced in almost fifty editions between the year of its publication and Keble's death in 1866. In an appendix to King's last charge to his clergy as bishop of Lincoln, 'King printed some seventy-five quotations from the Patristic literature given in Mr. Keble's Book entitled *Considerations*'.[14]

Keble had grown up in the Gloucestershire countryside with a deep love of natural beauty and an appreciation of plants and flowers and the changing seasons. In many ways Keble, whose faith had been molded by the teaching of his High Church father, is effectively the bridge between the High Church tradition of the great Caroline Divines, notably Andrewes and Hooker, of the seventeenth century, and the later Oxford Movement of the nineteenth century.

Although, unlike King, Keble was a distinguished scholar, with a double first-class degree from Corpus Christi College, Oxford, yet the two men were equally notable for their holiness of life and their emphasis upon pastoral care and Christian formation, although, in the case of Keble, not as a bishop, but as a country parish priest for thirty years in the Hampshire village of Hursley. Prior to his time as a country parson, he had been elected Professor of Poetry in the University of Oxford, a post he held for just four years before he returned to his much-loved countryside in Hursley, where he had originally served his title as a curate.

Keble has an advantage over the likes of Wordsworth in that Keble was both a poet, a theologian and a patristic scholar of great distinction. He was deeply involved together with Newman, Pusey and others in the publication of the early Fathers of both the Eastern and Western Churches, contributing to the *Tracts of the Times*, notably in Tract LXXXIX: *On the Mysticism attributed to the Early Fathers of the Church.* He was further schooled in the works of the Caroline Divines, with particular reference to Andrewes and Hooker, both of whom featured so prominently, not only in the writings of Pusey and Newman, but also in the notes we have of King's *Pastoral Lectures* and his other writings.

But it was in Keble's *Lectures on Poetry* where this is all drawn together, all of a piece—poetry, patristics and pastoral care—and always, in the case of Keble, as of King, with characteristic modesty and understatement at every turn of the page. Keble suggests:

> The Romantic poets proclaim a depth in the natural order which is neglected by the scientific investigator, in the same way as the Fathers discern a depth in scripture by their typological and allegorical interpretation. The Romantic poets, by reminding their readers of the mystery of creation, are a safeguard against an idolatry of the material world. In a similar way, the Fathers free us from the imprisonment of the letter to enable us to live in the presence of the mystery of God's working of our salvation.[15]

Keble saw Hooker's sacramentalism as exemplifying the theological understanding of the early Fathers, and the Christian Platonism of the Greek Fathers in particular, which so influenced the unbroken thread of the Anglican tradition, clearly and freshly emerging in the spirituality of the Oxford Movement and King in particular.

So Keble writes:

> The moral and devotional writings of the Fathers show that they were deeply imbued with the evangelical sentiment that Christians as such are living in a new heaven and a new earth; that to them 'old things are passed away', and 'all things are becoming new'; that the very

inanimate creation itself also is 'delivered from the bondage of corruption into the glorious liberty of the children of God'. Thus, in a manner, they seem to have realized, though in an infinitely higher sense, the system of Plato: everything to them existed in two worlds: the world of sense, according to its outward nature and relations; in the world intellectual according to its spiritual associations. And thus did the whole scheme of material things, and especially those objects in it which are consecrated by scriptural allusions, assume in their eyes a sacramental or symbolical character.[16]

Also in *The Christian Year*, Keble writes:

> Two worlds are ours: 'tis only Sin
> Forbids us to descry
> The mystic heaven and earth within
> Plain as the sea and sky.

Furthermore, from his patristic studies, Keble perceived that for the early Fathers of the Church, the omniscient God was 'so much in all their thoughts, that what to others would have been mere symbols, were to them designed expressions of His Truth, providential intimations of His will. In this sense, the whole world to them was full of sacraments.'[17]

A WORLD FULL OF SACRAMENTS

Although King clearly had neither the theological nor the scholarly acumen of Keble to pull all this together as a patristics scholar or as a published poet, nevertheless it is demonstrably evident, at every turn of the page in such as we do have of King's writings as well as of what others of his contemporaries have written about him, that King embodied, and not only in his teaching and preaching, this larger vision to which Keble frequently alludes and which was experienced in centuries past, by Isaiah in the Temple, of an earth, as well as of an heaven being 'full of the glory of God' (Isaiah 6:3).

It would seem that King came to this same cosmic sacramental vision, as it might be termed, not so much by the route of scholarship but, as he was at pains to point out in that opening address to the bishops at the Lambeth Conference of 1897, already quoted above, from 'the source of his own experience'. For King, such a sacramental world view, like so much else, was learned and garnished not from books, or only from books, but from his experience and by holding together what religion and philosophy tend to separate out into categories; stopping short (that well-worn formula yet again) with the covenanted sacrament or sacraments of the Church, but failing to press on further and beyond, and thereby so allowing the particular to point further to the general; the assurance of the Creator's Presence *somewhere*, to open our limited vision to that same Presence *everywhere*.

In one of his last annual letters to the nurses of the Guild of St Barnabas, King concludes with a quotation from Keble's *Christian Year* which in a few words draws together in a single vision the whole created

order, as pointing sacramentally to the Person of the
Creator, with what Augustine would have spoken
of as the 'eyes of the heart'.

> Thou Who hast given me eyes to see
> And love this sight so fair,
> Give me a heart to find out Thee
> And read Thee everywhere.[18]

For how you see, is what you see and in the case
of King his sacramental perspective was most certainly not confined or restricted to the specific sacraments of the Church or even to the quasi-sacramental method as being a way of reading scripture.
While King, as previously quoted,[19] unashamedly
asserted that 'there is a society called the Church,
claiming to be the covenanted sphere of the Divine
love', yet he immediately qualifies that by adding,
in parentheses, that nevertheless, the Church is 'not
the *exclusive* sphere, not hindering God from working elsewhere' but simply 'promising that we shall
find him there'.

So for King, everything and everyone and 'elsewhere' carried something of the signature of the
divine within, hidden except to those with the eyes
of the heart, revealed through parable or symbol,
perceived by faith and from a sacramental perspective. For 'faith perishes if it is walled in or confined.
If it is anywhere, it must be everywhere, like God
himself: if God is in your life, he is in all things, for he
is God. You must be able to spread the area of your
recognition for him and the basis of your conviction
about him, as widely as your thought will range.'[20]

It was precisely King's sacramental perspective on the whole of life which enabled him 'to spread the area of his recognition' of God 'everywhere' in the whole created order, resulting in an awakening of the senses.

THE SACRAMENTS AND THE SACRAMENTAL PERSPECTIVE

It's as though such an awakening to such a universal awareness of God's presence 'at all times and in all places' marks the end of religion in its usual sense with its demarcation and dividing lines of doctrine and dogma to be replaced by a sacramental world-view, as Alexander Schmemann suggests. In fact Schmemann goes further by claiming that 'religion is only needed where there is a wall of separation between God and man. But Christ who is both God and Man, has broken down the wall between God and man, He has inaugurated a new life, not a new religion.'[21]

Both King and the Fathers of the Oxford Movement reclaimed something of this insight from their patristic studies, especially from the Eastern Fathers. The spirituality of the Eastern Orthodox Churches as recent authors are clearly demonstrating, has managed to hold together an understanding of both the specifically 'covenanted' (as King puts it) sacraments of the Church, while at the same time extending a broader sacramental theology to include the whole created order, with an implied new respect and reverence for creation.

> The idea of sacramentality extends beyond the
> formal sacraments such as Baptism, Matrimony,
> Communion, and the Anointing of the Sick.
> This sense of sacramentality, rooted in the
> Incarnation, extends our vision out of the world
> so that everything can be a sacrament, meaning
> every person, creature, plant, and object can be
> an opportunity to encounter something of the
> Divine Presence in the world. Sacramentality
> is a quality present in creation that opens us up
> to the Sacred Presence in all things. Sacraments
> reveal grace.[22]

The seventh century St Isaac the Syrian goes further yet, by defining a charitable human heart as one 'which is burning with love for the whole creation, for humans, for the birds, for the beasts, for the demons—for all creation'.[23]

There is a wonderful saying attributed to Jesus which expresses the reality of God's presence everywhere: 'Lift up the stone and there thou shalt find me, cleave the wood and I am there.'[24]

Yet, although King would not have been so explicit theologically in his writings or teaching, he does not dodge the question when he asks:

> How are we to regard all this wonderful and
> beautiful world in which we find God has placed
> us, and which we believe that he has created?
> How are we to regard our Lord's command to
> consider the lilies of the field and the fowls of
> the air? How is it that our Lord based so much

of His teaching on the works of Nature? Why
did He so constantly invite those whom He was
teaching to look at and think about the visible
things of this world, as we see them, round
about us? The sower, the tares, the leaven, the
net, the lilies, the sparrows falling, the look of
the sky at morning and evening; in these and
many ways the Saviour calls our attention to the
things that are seen. This is no new difficulty,
but it is of very great importance. We should
consider it well, and obtain the true answer.

King continues by pointing out that many years
ago the great St Augustine had considered the same
question, to which he 'made a very simple but true
and beautiful reply':

> 'Perchance someone will say, heaven, earth, the
> sea and the moon and the stars, the beauties
> of the sky are in the world, and God made
> them, why should not I love that which God
> has made?'
> 'Well,' he replied, 'God forbids not that you
> should love them, but he forbids that you should
> so love them as to find in them your bliss. It
> is as if a spouse should give his betrothed a
> fair and precious ring, and if she to whom the
> ring was given should love the gift more than
> the giver. Would not her heart be convicted of
> unfaithfulness, even though that which she
> loved were her lover's gift? If she said in her
> heart, 'His gifts are enough for me, I care not
> to see his face,' where were her true love? The
> spouse gives the gift for this end that he himself
> may be the more beloved in it.' This is surely
> the true way of looking at the beauty of created
> things.[25]

THE OUTER VEIL AND THE INNER MEANING

And so it is, when 'viewed through this expansive lens, we discover that the more we cultivate intimacy with the natural world, the more we discover about God's presence. All of our interactions with nature can be sacramental, and all the ways nature extends herself to us are sacramental as well. Sacramentality breaks through our surface obsessions in the world and plunges us into the depth of the sacred at every turn'[26] — through the outer veil and into the inner meaning.

> We must be continually . . . growing in spiritual understanding, and interpretation of the things around us in this world, reading through the outer veil and seeing the inner meaning. We may enjoy the good things which God has given us, if we are living with the peculiar separateness which the saints of God should live in. We shall be gaining a greater independence of the things of sense.[27]

In seeking that 'true way of looking at the beauty of created things', King is explicit in the advice he gives in his teaching on the spiritual life. 'We must be growing in spiritual understanding, and interpretation of the things around us, in this world, reading through the outer veil and seeing the inner meaning.'[28]

Isaac Watts (1674–1748), as an almost exact contemporary of Wordsworth, and as a prolific Non-conformist hymn writer from a vastly different theological stable from that of either Keble or King, nevertheless eloquently captures this unitive world view, although he himself would never have held to anything of a theology of the sacraments of the Church. For Watts it is more his awakened inner life of the Spirit and his intense love of God as written up in his book of that same title—*Discourses of the Love of God*—which opened up for him that non dualistic vision of the contemplative life.

> The soul that loves God is ready to see and take notice of God in everything: he walks through the fields, he observes the wonders of divine workmanship in every different tree on his right hand and on his left, in the herbs and flowers that he treads with his feet, in the rich diversity of shapes and colours and ornaments of nature: he beholds and admires his God in them all. He sees the birds in their airy flight, or perched upon the branches, and sending forth their various melody: he observes the grazing of the flocks, and the larger cattle in their different forms and manners of life; he looks down upon little insects, and takes notice of their vigorous and busy life and motions, their shining bodies, and their golden or painted wings, he beholds and he admires his God in them all: in the least things of nature, he can read the greatness of God, and it is what of God he finds in the creature that renders creatures more delightful to him. Creatures are but his steps to help him to rise toward God.[29]

'What is fascinating about Watts is his capacity like Augustine', and moreover King, '*both* to celebrate the wonder of creation *and* to go far beyond that creation in order to reverence the wonder of his Creator: the point for both writers, is that creation has no value *except* in so far as it points beyond itself to its Creator.'[30]

Such is similarly true of King and also equally so of Bishop Sailer of Regensburg, one of King's great theological and spiritual mentors, and whose prolific writings King had devoured and expounded in his teaching during his Oxford days as pastoral professor: 'Sailer was a sort of genius' says King in one of his many letters to the nurses of the Guild of St Barnabas. 'He not only had some knowledge, but his mind saw the relation of things—how one thing touches another, around, below, and above: and so his mind has that kind of freshness, and strength, and gentleness, and simplicity and depth, which follow from being in touch with the circle of the One Truth.'[31]

PANTHEISM

Of course institutional religion is always somewhat suspicious of much that contemplatives and mystics have spoken or written of concerning such a unitive world view. Certainly King, as we shall see, was cautious about the contemporary growing interest in mysticism in his day, if, as King would have put it, it 'stops short' at what is seen or perceived superficially with the senses in outward appearance with a worship which is in danger of degenerating into the idolatry of pantheism. If there is no more of God than what is visible and tangible in the creation, then we are simply left with pantheism. The incarnate risen Christ together with our humanity ascends beyond the limits of time and space, leaving behind himself trails of glory in all that he has metaphorically touched.

It took that subversive vision of Peter in Joppa, for him to tear down the walls of division between what religion had deemed 'clean' or 'unclean', or the walls of separation between those deemed as inside the covenant and those 'outsiders', namely the Gentiles. Such a vision marks the end of religion as usually understood, cautioning theologians or philosophers not to fragment all that God has 'touched' in the Incarnation of Christ, by dividing the unclean from the clean, secular from sacred, or even what is usually termed as 'earthly' from the 'heavenly', both of which are perceived, as in that vision of Isaiah, as being 'full of his glory'.

> For the material wonders and beauties of this world are object lessons intended to teach us something higher and more wonderful than themselves. This, St Paul tells us plainly, is the right view, 'For the invisible things of Him from the creation of the world are clearly seen, being understood by the things that are made, even His eternal Power and Godhead.' And this is surely the way in which the Blessed Saviour taught us to consider the works of Nature, the lilies of the field and the fowls of the air, ever pointing us onward and upward to think of the

things in the Kingdom of Grace. The parables point to something more than the natural eye can see; the voices of Nature mean more than the natural ear can hear. This is surely the spirit of the oft-repeated saying of our Lord, 'He that hath ears to hear, let him hear.' [32]

So King is clear that the lilies of the field and the parables 'point to something more than the natural eye can see', to the God who is both in his creation, but also beyond creation. Pantheism is the restricted and limited view, 'stopping short' with what is seen within the limitations of the world, while *panentheism* points us both to the God in the world as well as to the God beyond, who transcends his Creation, perceived as always by those 'with eyes to see and ears to hear'—for those who are fully awakened and attentive: the poets and artists, the mystics and contemplatives of the world.

REAWAKENING TO
A SACRAMENTALLY RECHARGED VISION

Every generation, and surely not least our own, will always be in need of such a further fine tuning of the ears of the heart to hear this same theme, albeit in a different key, if it is not to be deafened to the subtleties of the wisdom of this non-dualistic 'message' by that side of the brain which consistently prefers to divide, in order to control. In every generation this will require nothing less than a recurrent spiritual re-awakening.

In a sermon about Jacob and his dream, King with that characteristic simplicity and depth, says: 'All we have to do is to awaken like Jacob from a dream, and admit that this world is still the House of God: that the Lord is even in this place, though we knew it not.'[33]

The close association between the Oxford Movement and not least the person and influence of King and the whole Romantic Movement, not only in art and architecture but notably in the works of the Romantic poets, all served to recapture the imagination of the culture of the times. Keble, in his *Lectures on Poetry* firmly believed that the poet and the man of faith share a common conviction that there is more to life than what meets the eye, that we are part of a greater whole than we can fully recognize, and in that way to reawaken a latent sacramental world view.

> Those who, from their very heart, either burst into poetry, or seek the Deity in prayer, must needs ever cherish with their whole spirit the vision of something more beautiful, greater and more lovable, than all that mortal eye can see. Thus the very practice and cultivation of Poetry will be found to possess, in some sort, the power and guiding and composing of the mind to worship and prayer.[34]

So, in revisiting the spirituality of King and others, it becomes increasingly evident how very much we need the poets and the envisioned prophets to recapture for our own age that spirituality which fuels the imagination of both heart and mind, so as to rescue us from that consumerism and materialism which are so blind to what is hidden of the Divine within the material world of nature and of our humanity, rather than continuing to sleep walk and to use and abuse the created order for our own selfish ends. Neither new laws nor informed education alone can save our planet or indeed the human race from tragic self-destruction.

> The tragic separation between grace and nature, between the spiritual and the physical, that has dominated so much of our Western Christian inheritance and made room for the Western world's unchecked exploitation and abuse of nature. We urgently need to awaken again to the reintegration of the spiritual and the physical, if we are to begin to reverse the threat to planetary existence as we have known it.[35]

There is much talk today of the need to revisit this re-envisioned perspective so intrinsic to the Celtic tradition which is to be found in the likes of Patrick, Cuthbert and Aidan and other Celtic saints who in their day were clearly so attentive to the harmonies of the Creator orchestrated in the very fabric of the material world of the whole created order. There is no evidence in anything we have of King of any reference to that Celtic tradition as such. Rather, King, along with the Fathers of the Oxford Movement trace this same theme from the Neo-Platonism of Augustine, to whom King consistently makes reference in his preaching and teaching alike, as well as together with the Eastern Fathers with their doctrine of *theosis* and *divinization*.

Yet, whatever can resource a return to a renewed unitive worldview with both its responsibilities and opportunities, urgently needs to be reclaimed in today's schizoid world, for 'to know that spirit and matter are interwoven, that heaven and earth, the divine and the human are inseparably intertwined, is to know also that what we do to matter, matters. In the Celtic world' — as in King's world view and the world viewed as sacrament — 'to adore the divine is to reverence the human, to love heaven is to cherish the earth, and to celebrate spirit is to honour matter. And it is to do all these things with compassion, by bringing the heart of our being into faithful relationship with the heart of one another's being and allowing the interrelationship of all things to guide us and to inspire us in how we live and act.'[36]

It is not accidental that the theology implicit in Wordsworth and the poets of the Romantic movement together with the poetry of Keble and the immense personal influence of King all alike, although drawing on different resources, paved the way for the ideological and philosophical undergirding of the Arts and Crafts Movement in people like John Ruskin and William Morris, as well as for the Christian Socialist Movement, with its heroic slum priests like Lowder, Mackonochie and Stanton, who were so devoted to working with the poor in the oppressive urbanization of the Industrial Revolution. Intrinsic to all those socially radical movements and persons is—at least implicitly, if not explicitly—a re-evaluation of the material world, of nature and the environment and of the value and respect owed to ever member of the human race. It is like so much throughout this narrative, as needing urgently to recapture a whole world view which is all of a piece, as evidenced and experienced in the contemplative life, graced by contemplative prayer.

5

Contemplative Prayer
and the Contemplative Life

*Personal devotedness to a personal God is one of the
chief marks of a true religion.*[1]

THE PRESENCE AND POWER OF GOD

Although King would seldom, if ever, have used
the term 'contemplative prayer', or indeed spoken
of the 'contemplative life' as such, his insistence on
the need for times spent consciously alone and in
communion with God in personal prayer and meditation, are the constant and persistent themes of his
teaching and preaching, as well as in his letters of
spiritual direction to clergy and laity alike. He speaks
of this, as he always speaks, not so much from what
he has learned from books, but rather from experience, and not so much in technical terms, but rather
with 'simplicity and depth'.

'Wherein lies the secret of our strength and our
peace', King asks a group of ordinands on the eve
of their ordination? 'Wherein lies our real strength?'
And the reply, quite simply: 'It is in communion
with GOD.'

'Get times for special and deliberate communion with GOD; your prayers, your Bible, and the Blessed Sacrament will be the great normal occasions, and you will find it also to be a great help if you can attend a Retreat or Quiet Day every year: "Be still then and know that I am God", the Psalmist says.' And then in that frequently recurring reference, in letters and lectures alike—*vacare considerationi*—'get time to try St Bernard's advice to his kind friend, Pope Eugenius'.[2]

To spell that out, King quotes from his favourite priest poet, John Keble:

> Mr. Keble speaks of that 'deep silence in the heart, for thought to do her part'. All teach us the same truth, the value of retirement, silence in solitude, in order that we may realize more the Presence and Power of GOD.[3]

Without this there is always the danger of Christian discipleship degenerating into a formalism unless, constantly renewed and resourced by the inner life of the transforming Spirit of the Risen and Ascended Christ.

On another occasion in a sermon in the University Church in Oxford, he extemporizes on the same theme:

> He who made us and has redeemed us, said: 'If a man love me. He will keep my words, and my Father will love him, and we will come unto him and make our abode with him.' Personal devotedness to a personal God is one of the chief marks of a true religion. The Bible calls it

walking with God. Christianity in its essential working, is not a religion of detachment, but of attachment; a religion not of fear, but of love. It is the assurance of the companionship of a Friend always able and willing to guide, check, and support us in all dangers.

And then, as always with King, the point is driven home by speaking out of what is clearly his own personal experience to validate and give authority to his words:

All this is no mere language of theoretical theology, or excited devotional feeling, but may be the sure experience of our daily lives.[4]

THREEFOLD PATTERN: CORPORATE WORSHIP
AND PERSONAL PRAYER

For King, both corporate worship in the liturgy, together with scripture whether as in the Daily Offices or personal Bible study, require that third element of personal prayer in times of silence and solitude in order to interiorize what otherwise can degenerate into formalism and even superficiality.

'The New Testament gives the threefold pattern which is at the heart of all Catholic practice: Eucharist–Office–personal devotion.'[5] Such are the ingredients of a healthy spirituality, which as well as being clearly King's spirituality are demonstrably also the constituent elements of the spirituality of the Book of Common Prayer which itself is also essentially

A Love Surpassing Knowledge

the spirituality of St Benedict. 'Here is the basic Rule of the Church', maintains Martin Thornton, 'which, varying in detail, is common to East and West, monastic and secular, to all the individual schools without exception.'[6]

It was this same three-fold pattern which was embedded in the daily timetable of King's Cuddesdon from its earliest days (although a place was not provided in the timetable for silent prayer and meditation until 1875), and clearly such was the pattern of King's daily life and the foundation of his spirituality, summarized in King's own words—'the supernatural power of prayer, the supernatural power of the revealed Word, the supernatural power of the Sacraments'.[7]

There can be no question that, although King's 'style' in so many respects differed markedly from that of Liddon in the early years when Liddon was vice-principal of Cuddesdon, nevertheless, both men would have agreed for the need for such a pattern, as a framework for a rule of life, albeit adapted for particular persons and in differing circumstances.

King, however—though perhaps with less rigidity than that which characterized Liddon's teaching and practice—saw the need for a balance of head and heart, doctrine and devotion, corporate worship and personal prayer, while nonetheless also emphasizing the importance of times set apart for personal communion with God in solitude and the hidden life of the Spirit. It is that practice and discipline which generally speaking is the first of the three elements to be discarded in over-busy lives preoccupied with good works.

Preaching at the dedication of the new chapel for the Bishop's Hostel in Lincoln in 1907,[8] King opens his heart by returning to this constant theme of 'personal communion with God' or specifically 'Jesus' on this particular occasion, as affording 'the opportunity of studying His ways, listening to His teaching, and opportunities of observing its naturalness, its simplicity in the parables as He drew them from the ordinary passing events of the day, and then the privilege of being instructed in their deeper meaning when the disciples were alone with him in the house.' In everything the first priority, as King persistently maintained, is the need to 'secure our own individual re-union with God through Christ', nurtured in those times apart, in solitude and silence.

The young, rather High-Church Stanton, in a letter to Liddon who had been his confessor during his time as an undergraduate at Oxford, expressed his disappointment on arriving at Cuddesdon with the principal, who at that time was the saintly Swinny. From the perspective of the young Stanton's churchmanship, Swinny's churchmanship was somewhat lower down the candle to that of his own, or indeed to that of Liddon. However Liddon's reply to the young Stanton is worthy of note. After some reassuring words to the young ordinand, Liddon continues:

> If the system of the College does not yield all that you could imagine or wish, you will feel that it does at least afford very many opportunities

for growth in holiness . . . All the real work—
all that will last—must be wrought alone—on
your knees—and with God. Compared with
the great question of growth in habits of private
prayer—whether mental or vocal—the little
external matters are not of great importance.[9]

At the outset of his brief time as principal of Cuddesdon, Swinny was known to be a man of 'moderate' opinions in matters of churchmanship, However, as is often the case, he undoubtedly grew into the job, during his time as principal. 'He arrived at the College distrustful of the system of worship, the frequent services. He gradually became convinced of their value. He learnt to understand what was meant by meditation' and the importance of it. In a letter to King in the summer of 1861, he wrote:

I preached on Wednesday on Meditation. I
grow more and more in the conviction of its
importance. We all try to do too much and don't
give time enough to earnest quiet thought. I
know the case is my own. Somehow even prayer,
and Divine service with God's congregation,
lose much of their reality without this deliberate
bringing of the Unseen into sight, and basking
in the Light and Warmth of it for a little season.
We shall accomplish more by attempting less.[10]

Clearly Swinny here is playing back to King what King had always championed as well as practised in his own life, concerning the importance of that third ingredient of making time for personal prayer alone, consciously in the presence of God through the indwelling of the Holy Spirit of the Risen Lord.

Of course at that stage, both for Swinny as for Cuddesdon, 'meditation' would mean mental prayer, or discursive prayer along Ignatian lines. And such was the core teaching of Liddon. Such a time of prayer was rooted in meditating on a passage of scripture, clothing it and enlivening it 'by reverent imaginations'. Then the understanding should work upon the picture of the chosen passage until the intellect 'retires', its function ended. 'The point upon which it has fixed as cardinal is transferred to the will.'[11]

In this way, Liddon stressed, how the specific time for prayer gives way, spontaneously and freely throughout the rest of the day, in the course of 'the daily round and common task', to moments of ejaculatory prayer 'rising spontaneously to the throne of God', 'culling from Holy Scripture or the Prayer Book some choice and piercing words'.[12]

Much of this would have been what King sought to convey to those he taught concerning a right reading of scripture, by not 'stopping short' (to use that recurring phrase of King, which he applies to all the means of Grace) with the written word speaking as it tends to do to the intellect, but then, to go on and be directed to the living Word—the person of Christ to whom the scriptures point. It is in that way that conceptual knowledge is transcended in a relationship of love, for as St Paul cautioned: 'Knowledge puffs up, love builds up' (I Corinthians 8:1) as a love that surpasses knowledge.

A Love Surpassing Knowledge

KNOWLEDGE AND LOVE

King was always insistent that the wrong kind of knowledge—knowledge restricted to information located only in the intellect or left hemisphere of the brain, with the resulting imbalance of head and heart—can inhibit true prayer. Again, when addressing ordinands:

> At the present time we need seriously to consider the true end and object of knowledge . . . Modern knowledge, the knowledge which is in such demand at the present day, is in great danger of being divorced from the knowledge and love of God . . . [There is a danger now] of becoming entangled in the veil of knowledge divorced from faith. We do well to acquire knowledge, but we ought to remember to look beyond and above.[13]

This echoes some words of St Bernard, with whom King was certainly well acquainted:

> There are those who seek knowledge for the sake of knowledge; that is curiosity. There are those who seek knowledge to be known by others; that is vanity. There are those who seek knowledge in order to serve: that is love.

It is abundantly clear from such as we have of King's writings, and especially from the notes of his *Pastoral Lectures*, that he was exceptionally well acquainted not only with the writings of St Bernard, but also with the writings of St Augustine, frequently recommending both of them to his students.

'Central to Augustine's theology is the relation between knowledge and love, or if it is preferred, between reason and revelation.'[14] And such a synthesis is equally true of St Anselm on whom King also draws for much of his pastoral and ascetical theology and, as we have seen, it is to St Anselm that we go for the roots of anything that might exemplify the English school of spirituality.

> One of the strange contrasts of Anselm's richly-dowered mind consists in having given expression with inexorable rigour to the rights of divine justice, while at the same time he succeeds in describing in touching terms the delights of the love of God . . . To study him makes us better, for nowhere else do we find knowledge so completely transformed into love.[15] Ditto, ditto—Edward King!

Although it is difficult to find in any of the writings we have from King on specific teaching about personal prayer and meditation, except a few passing references to what the Middle Ages termed *lectio divina* as being the way of reading scripture, and pointing from the written word to the Living Word, without 'stopping short', King consistently refers to this intimate relationship with the Person of Christ as being that of an intimate Friend and Companion.

> Man is no longer left alone, plodding on the path of duty in obedience to a law within, but he has risen above the law, to the Lawgiver, he has found a Companion, a Friend—the personal God.[16]

King persistently saw the danger of 'stopping short', as he repeatedly used to speak of it, with the outward forms of religion—the Church, the Bible and the Sacraments—rather than growing and 'daily increasing' in the inner life of the Spirit. 'Humanity', King insisted, 'was taken into personal union with the Godhead by the Incarnation, not absorbed or destroyed, and the fruits of the Incarnation are, in the case of most of us, certainly far less than they might be.'

Yet as King realized: 'This is the great step which some still seem unable to take—the step of obedience to a moral law' (the Old Covenant), 'to communion with the personal God; to step from *a* commandment to *Thy* commandment'. For, as King was so very eager to point out:

> There is always the danger of substituting the Church, or the ministry, or the mere use of the Sacraments for the individual realization of personal communion with the one personal God; that men may put the Bible, their own faith, or feelings, in the place of God, and loose half-unconsciously, the real end for which our Faith and the Bible are given—a full knowledge and love of the Person and Life of Jesus.[17]

DOCTRINE AND DEVOTION

Repeatedly, both in references to Bishop Sailer of Regensberg, one of King's several mentors, as well as in King's own teaching and preaching, the balance of head and heart is urged. Knowledge and love, or head and heart need to be held in balance if we are to discover that rounded and balanced fullness of life which we see in the perfect union of the human and the divine in the person of the Christ of God. Indeed, by the Holy Spirit and the transforming process of gentle 'loving correction' (yet another phrase especially dear to King) matures into the fullness of life in Christ—'being changed from one degree of glory to another' (II Corinthians 3:18) so that what Christ has begun in each of us, he may continue by perfecting in us.

Devotion will go astray if it is not bridled by doctrine, and divine learning, and, if it is truly incarnational, it must lead into affective prayer of the heart, since when fully understood, reason and love are two parts of one thing and need to ride in tandem without either side dominating the other. William of St Thierry to whom King frequently referred in his pastoral lectures, in his *Enigma of Faith*, which is virtually a treatise on this very point of the need to balance affective devotion of the heart and theology, demonstrates them as essentially interacting with one another.

> Charity, is the soul's natural light, and was created by the Author of Nature for seeing God. There are two eyes to this spiritual vision, forever straining to see the light which is God, and their names are Love and Reason . . . these two help each other—reason instructs love, and love enlightens reason. Reason merges into affectivity, and love consents to be limited

by reason. Then it is that they can achieve great
things.[18]

King would have found in the writings of William of
St Thierry so much of that balance and affective-spec-
ulative synthesis of head and heart which he saw in
the writings of Bishop Sailer of Regensburg, from
whom he drew so much in his own teaching as well
as also exemplifying in his own spirituality. Furthermore, it was precisely this balance that was needed as
a corrective in the age of the Enlightenment. Indeed,
we can venture further and affirm such teaching
as being necessary in demolishing 'three errors' of
which religion must be consistently aware in any age,
and of which William of St Thierry was so concerned
to address in his *Mirror of Faith.*

> The first is narrow 'spirituality', prayer divorced
> from the rest of life; the second, a lazy quest for
> a 'simple' faith, seen as something comfortably
> static and almost the direct opposite to hard-
> won 'simplicity'; the third, intellectualism, the
> pastoral ideal of merely 'instructed' Christians.
> Against all this, *The Mirror of Faith* could be
> the *locus classicus* of the ascetical approach; of
> supporting theological thinking against merely
> knowing a lot of theology.[19]

Louis Bouyer summarizes this whole necessary synthesis:

> Faith will never be what it ought to be if it
> remains an abstract conception of the mind. The
> whole and entire man must be unreservedly
> involved in his acceptance of the truth.[20]

It is precisely in the 'work' of personal prayer, and by transcending words, that God receives the 'green light' to continue *in* us his saving work which he has once and for all, in the Paschal Mystery, done *for* us, in the ongoing process of the Word continuing to be enfleshed in our humanity and person. Vernacular scripture, emphasis on recollection rather than formal private prayer, and meditation rather than extra-liturgical devotions, are direct developments from the whole fourteenth-century practice of the English school of spirituality and clearly evident in King.

THEOLOGY AND SPIRITUALITY: DOCTRINE AND DEVOTION

So, concludes King:

> While our faculties are taken up into communion with the Divine, the companionship of God becomes a reality of our daily life, and our 'exceeding great reward'. And then besides, and with all this, we have the special consciousness of communion with the Incarnate Word. 'Jesus Christ, the same yesterday, today and forever': and being so, we know what to do and where to find Him.[21]

'Where to find him'? King's answer to that, is simply to follow through from the promise of Christ to 'abide in us' with the realization that we also may abide in Him.

Here again, with King, it's a matter of words clearly spoken from experience:

> As we advance in years, we see that the real point for care and anxiety is not so much the saying our prayers (though they still have to be said), as the *abiding* in the spiritual condition which is essential for the full efficacy of prayer: 'If you abide in me, and my words abide in you, ask whatsoever ye will, and it shall be done unto you' (St John 15: 7). What must be, then, our chief prayer? Surely this, that we may ourselves abide in Christ more truly than we do.[22]

'Communion with the Divine' or as in scripture, 'partakers in the divine nature', and yes, all of that and even in the here and now of daily life. The plan that is finished, accomplished and in that sense perfected, is the atoning work of Christ—'an at-one-ment, whereby all that is divided by sin is reconciled and made one in Christ who is at one with His Father and ours—so that all may be One'. Furthermore, and of no lesser importance—'not by losing the uniqueness of the parts, but by raising the parts to a greater identity within God'.

In typical 'simplicity and depth' King expounds this doctrine in one of his spiritual letters:

> Man would not look up to God, so God came down to man, and walked before him, and with him, and attended him in his daily life, that leading him to Himself He might in the end carry him up to God.[23]

In the Orthodox Churches of the East, this is known

as *theosis* or *divinization.* Although there is no direct reference to either of these doctrines in anything we have of King, there is no doubt that he, along with the theology and spirituality of his fellow Tractarians, from experience if not from first hand acquaintance and at least in his advanced in years, was aware of this deepening of the inner life of the Spirit.

Although it would seem that *theosis* or *divinization* were not part of King's spiritual vocabulary, it is manifestly clear that such, in practice, is at the heart of both his experience and his theology of prayer.

MYSTICISM AND CONTEMPLATION

Another word which is somewhat conspicuous by its absence in King's vocabulary, is the word mysticism, which in many ways is not totally unrelated to the practice of contemplative prayer, or even the prayer of 'loving regard', as in many ways the practice of mysticism and contemplative prayer are closely related.

But for King, from what we know of him, it is fair to assume that perhaps there would have been something a bit too self-conscious or elitist about the actual word, or even the hint of an imbalance between prayer and social action with its accompanying tendency to quietism .

The word *mystica* entered the Christian vocabulary in the sixth century and became widely used only from the ninth century. Before that, the word used for the phenomenon we now call mysticism, was *contemplatio*. Within Christianity the word contemplation was used by Augustine, Gregory, Bernard (mystics who had no influence from Dionysius) and it is still the word more commonly used than the word for mysticism.

There is also the influence of the Christian fathers—Augustine and Gregory and the rest. Then there is Bernard of Clairvaux (1090–1153), the last of the fathers, whose sermons on the Song of Songs were to have such a great impact on all subsequent mystical theology. In the mysticism which flourished in this medieval period the whole emphasis is on love.

> In a theological framework, mystical experience was interpreted as follows: God who is love infuses his gift of love into the soul. When man responds to this call, he receives the Holy Spirit who is love personified. Writers of the time (including Thomas Aquinas) quote that text of the Fourth Gospel which says that love calls down the Holy Spirit: 'If you love me you will keep my commandments. And I will pray the Father and he will give you another Counsellor to be with you for ever, even the Spirit of Truth.'[24]

During the thirteenth and fourteenth centuries, schools of mysticism had flourished in the centres of spirituality and learning which arose within the great religious orders. There were Benedictine, Cistercian, Franciscan schools, as well as the so-called Victorines—Richard and Hugh to whom King specifically refers—'a group of theologians associated with the Abbey of Saint-Victor in Paris, fondly known as the Victorines'. (*The Four Degrees of Passionate Charity* by Richard de St Victor would most certainly have been known by King.) Also, and at about the same time there was a whole cluster of English mystics, notably Julian of Norwich, Walter Hilton and the anonymous author of *The Cloud of Unknowing*, although none of these are referred to specifically in anything we have of King.

Towards the close of the nineteenth century and during the last years of King's life, there was a marked revival of interest in mysticism, with people like Dean Inge appointed to St Paul's in 1911 and Evelyn Underhill, who wrote and published her large book entitled *Mysticism* in that same year,1911, only one year after King's death. At about the same time, Forbes Robinson, the remarkable chaplain of Christ's College, Cambridge was beginning to conduct Retreats and Quiet Days on mysticism. A lady wrote to King in the summer of 1904, sending a copy of Forbes Robinson's *Addresses*. In writing to thank her for the gift, he raises some tentative cautions about the whole practice of mysticism.

> There is a great deal that is most inspiring; indeed, the whole of his personality and tone of mind is so. And I hope to keep it by me to keep me up on the high spiritual level. There is just one caution, I venture to think, needed. It is a characteristic, much of that line of thought, the danger of running into a kind of Pantheism, I mean the danger of losing the self to the degree of extinction by absorption . . . It was the danger

of Quietism, and even Fenelon was thought to
have sympathized with it too much. No doubt
most of us are only too far the other way, and
are only beginning to see the perfection of the
individual through the 'corporate union' in the
Godhead.[25]

His concluding words are most important because
they hold together in a theology of spirituality in
which union, communion and unity retain paradoxically their individual uniqueness: we become
more perfectly our unique selves by being in union
and relationship, the model of which is nothing less
than that of the unity of the Blessed Trinity, in whose
image, humanity is cast. So King concludes: 'I think
if one takes the highest possible standard, we have
the true safeguard: "*One as we* are one" — that is,
with the ineffable distinctions of the Three Divine
Personalities',[26] i.e. with each retaining their own
unique personhood.

We also find King, somewhat similarly cautious
about mysticism in the notes we have from his pastoral lectures, in the early years of his time as professor
of moral and pastoral theology in Oxford. King urges
his students:

Read the books of the mystics. Richard and
Hugh of St Victor — This would lead us up to
where it gets wrong — when people get to the
extreme of mysticism. Then comes in quietism
and spiritual apathy.[27]

King almost certainly would have known of Evelyn Underhill who, in the early years of her life had

found institutionalized religion and the formal worship of the Church not at all to her liking. It was only a decade or so later under the spiritual direction of Baron von Hügel, that she embraced Anglicanism, and later became a well-known Retreat Conductor and a much sought after spiritual director. In 1925, in a letter to someone who had sought her spiritual counsel and who, like Underhill herself, found institutional religion difficult:

> You aren't and never will be a real 'institutional soul' and are not required by God to behave like one. Your religion must of course have some institutional element, but it is particularly important that this element should not be overdone; and it certainly is not to be used as a penance.[28]

Dean Inge (1854–1941) of St Paul's calls the Fourth Gospel the charter of Christian mysticism: 'The Gospel of St John—the "spiritual gospel" as Clement calls it is the Charter of Christian mysticism . . . Perhaps, as Origen says, no one can fully understand it who has not, like its author, lain upon the breast of Jesus.'[29]

Although King in his teaching perhaps appears to be somewhat unnecessarily cautious or even condescending about the recovery of mysticism which had had similar influence in the English school of spirituality during the fourteenth and seventeenth centuries, he was clearly aware of this whole movement, at least in the later years of the nineteenth century and his own later life. He wrote in his penultimate

Christmas letter to the Guild of St Barnabas in 1908, only a little over a year from his death:

> Some forty years ago we were struggling in Oxford to maintain the very existence of 'Moral Truth'; now we have books on the highest stages of the moral and spiritual life, such as we were accustomed to look for in the mystical writers of the Middle Ages, and in other communions.[30]

The struggle to which King is referring in this letter and subsequently in the next and final letter of the following Christmas, 1909, and which he had expounded more fully back in 1897 in his Addresses to the Bishops at Lambeth, constitutes an important leap in his own spiritual journey. For the want of a better explanation, it might well have marked a development from mental and affective prayer to the more silent, wordless prayer of the contemplative and mystic. Such a development is not unusual in later life and generally requires guidance from a spiritual director to avoid the pitfalls of Quietism — clearly a pitfall of which King was well aware.

All this represents an enormous shift theologically from the deism of Paley's *Evidences* of the eighteenth century as well as philosophically from the reductionist and empiricist philosophy of John Locke and David Hume to the more optimistic Christian humanism and Idealism of the new Hegelians and in particular, to that of T. H. Green.

Although Green was not a paid up Christian, he is an essential bridge not only philosophically but also in the out workings of a theology with its high doctrine of the Incarnation and all that it came to imply for the great work of the slum priests and the Christian Socialists, with people like Charles Gore and Scott Holland, both of whom were close friends of King. Clearly Green had a great impact on King at every level, and not least at the level of King's own spiritual development experienced in discursive meditation to affective prayer of head and heart and ultimately in the fulfilment of that same spirituality in contemplative prayer and the contemplative life, with the latter as flowing from the former in social action.

SOCIAL ACTION

Some classical definitions of contemplation might suggest the contemplative life as being opposed to that of the active life, as when Thomas Aquinas in defining contemplation speaks of it as being 'a simple gaze on God and divine things proceeding from love and tending thereto' or again with St Francis de Sales for whom contemplation is 'a loving, simple and permanent attentiveness of the mind to divine things'. Yet in neither of these two cases was that so, and neither need it be so, for here again with regard to 'social action' we find in King that same balance between head and heart, prayer and life, the first and second commandment, contemplative prayer and the contemplative life which necessarily flows from it. Another way of expressing the same point:

> There will be times when the Spirit drives a
> person into the desert as He drove Jesus into
> the desert, and there will be other times when
> the same Spirit will drive the same person into
> the heart of action. Once again it is a question
> of discernment; once again it is a question of
> attentiveness to the voice of the beloved within.[31]

Yet, so far from contrasting the way of Mary with
that of Martha, or prizing either one as being higher
than the other, it is much more important to see the
way of Mary—Contemplative prayer—as resourc-
ing the life and directed energies of Martha—the
Contemplative life—in social action: the latter is not
over and against the former, but rather flows from
it. In that way, good deeds are resourced from the
sap of the deep roots of prayer and life in the Spirit
and are experienced as fruits of the Spirit. So the
contemplative way is certainly not, unless wrongly
understood, the way of escape. Furthermore, and
even for those called to the enclosed contemplative
life, such a life is drawn mystically into union with
the suffering and darkness of Calvary which is at
the very redemptive epicentre of the world's pain
and suffering, and furthermore, as mystically participating in the saving work of Christ.

'BISHOP OF THE POOR'

In a letter to Canon Ottley in 1885, commenting on
the choice of the Lincoln diocese to which he had

recently been appointed bishop, King wrote: 'I am glad it is John Wesley's diocese. I shall try to be the Bishop of the Poor.'[32]

And with that same pastoral zeal, to another he writes in his characteristic humility:

> I have, as you know, no great gifts, but, by God's goodness, I have a great and real love of His poor; and, if it should please Him to let me be the bishop of His poor and enable me to help them to see more what they are to Him and what He is to them, I think I shall be happy.[33]

Writing to his great friend and biographer, Randolph, in response to his letter congratulating King on his appointment to Lincoln: 'Now I am to go back to the Cure of souls, and be a shepherd again of the sheep and of the lambs. This is my great delight, and my hope, that God means it as a proof of His love, and that he means me to be a Bishop of His Poor! If I can keep that before me, I shall be happy.'[34]

Scott Holland, a lifelong friend of King, testifies of him:

> He loved the poor with a peculiar reverence and delight. He was their man. He knew them through and through. He felt as they felt. He could get to the heart of the very rough lads who were the bane of Wheatley and Cuddesdon.[35]

Here again, with King as we've already seen in so many aspects of his life and teaching, everything belongs together, his prayer and his daily life whether as a pastor or a teacher or a bishop—all are of a piece.

Here was no 'do-gooding' or a paternalistic patronizing; rather, it flowed out of the same heart as all his pastoral work, regardless of class or creed.

Wesley, for whom King had the very highest regard, notably declared — 'No Gospel but the social Gospel', and was certainly 'a lover of the poor and frequently made efforts to relieve them', although in the main 'he gave verbal support rather than taking fresh initiatives of his own for work or for campaigns in this area . . . Methodist philanthropy was a personal philanthropy and thus much less conspicuous than the large-scale philanthropic enterprises of the age.'[36]

Such a genuine love for the poor had always had a significant place in the spiritual revival of both the Evangelical Revival with the Clapham Sect as well as with the Tractarians and the Hackney Phalanx, and in both cases, largely lay led. Charles Marriott the great mentor of King during his time at Oriel, exemplified such a love and compassion for the poor to which King constantly referred throughout the whole of his life. The Rev'd John Day, who had tutored and influenced the young King prior to his going to Oriel, not only had this same care for the poor, but became a member of the Oddfellows Society, which for several centuries had existed as what was termed a 'Friendly Society' supporting the families and widows of working men in hard times. It should be no surprise therefore that King, shortly after his arrival in Lincoln, became a member of the Oddfellows Society.

Yet, as with Wesley, so with King whose passionate care and compassion for the poor would not have been perceived in the abstract as 'the problem of poverty' attached to an ideological source—whether to the left or the right politically—but from the solid theological foundation of his spirituality—that inner life of the Spirit which had deepened and developed with the passing of the years. And it is consistent: it is the theology of the Incarnation whereby, in our humanity we become partakers of Christ's divinity as he, once and for all, became and is ever more fully partaking in our humanity and the material world of his creation, as the cosmic Christ. Viewed from within time, we tend to refer to the Incarnation as a one-off event manifested in the Person of the Jesus of history two thousand years ago. However, more fully understood, the Incarnation is also an ongoing process until the Christ of faith 'is all in all', and in which we also, as 'workers together with God' (I Corinthians 3:9) have a crucial part to play.

And so in King's last letter to the nurses of the Guild of St Barnabas:

> Let this be your New Year's thought—'I am to carry on the great work of the incarnation'. This is no mere fancy, but the truth based upon the great words of Scripture, 'The Word became made flesh . . . And of his fullness have we all received.' Through the Incarnation God and man are linked together most mysteriously so that our Saviour says, 'In as much as ye did it unto one of the least of these my brethren, ye did it unto me.'[37]

And the source by which this can become a living reality is the contemplative way of life, which flows out of and is resourced by times of contemplative prayer in silence and solitude. In that way, the contemplative life flows directly from and is resourced by the contemplative prayer, as the energies of the interior life are expressed in what today we would term as social action, and again, here as elsewhere, it is essentially all of a piece, as in King's own words: 'The individual Churchman is also a citizen and must take his share in public service. We cannot reach our individual perfection without fulfilling our duties to others.'[38] And in conclusion to the nurses: 'Your prayers, your Bible and the Blessed Sacrament are the great means by which this precious truth is kept alive in your minds and hearts.'[39]

So often throughout history, the way of action and the way of contemplation have been seen in opposition, and an even more erringly, the way of contemplation is so often regarded as being superior to that of the active life. Mary, who sits lovingly, attentively and silently at the feet of Jesus is actually singled out as the model of Christian perfection while Martha, in the kitchen busily occupied with the pans and pans, is regarded as something of a second class disciple.

> This tradition is found in *The Cloud of Unknowing* which makes an unfortunate distinction between those called to perfection (and these are the contemplatives) and those called to salvation — and these are the actives. But Thomas Aquinas,

himself a Dominican friar, has more esteem for
action in what he calls the mixed life. Firstly,
because it is better for the candle to give light
than just to burn, and in the same way it is
better to share the fruit of contemplation than
just to contemplate. Secondly, this mixed life
was chosen by Jesus Christ—who taught and
preached and healed and lived an active life.
For Thomas, the eye of love gazes not only on
divine realities but also on human realities. Or,
more correctly, it sees the divine in the human:
it sees God in the world.[40]

Perhaps even more correctly, both contemplative
prayer and contemplative action derive from the
same source, for 'the eye of love gazes not only on
divine realities but also on human realities' —in the
poor, in my neighbour.

Seeing the divine in the human is the theological
and spiritual awareness which drives compassion for
the poor at the personal level rather than speaking
of the 'problem of poverty'. Likewise, 'seeing God in
the world' re-envisions our care for the environment
when the whole of the created world is perceived as
sacrament in the extended sense of the word. It was
with that same 'eye of love', that King perceived and
caught the vision of Isaiah in the temple, whereby
heaven *and* earth are full of the glory of God. It was
nothing less than that which motivated and ener-
gized King's own passionate love, both for the poor
as well as for the world of nature.

It is the eye of love of the contemplative as one of
'God's spies' to use Shakespeare's term, who sees in

others what so many with 'careless eyes' and without
the aid of the contemplative lens fail to see.

King, in one of his annual letters to the nurses of
the Guild of St Barnabas, elaborates on this whole
theme, and again by quoting from Wordsworth to
endorse his claim:

> Tender, loving care for poor, as well as rich, is a
> progress in hat inner penetration into the value
> of the mental, moral, and spiritual jewels which
> often lie concealed beneath the rough surface
> of working men and women, and which made
> Wordsworth speak with admiration and love
> of the characters of those whom he had met as
> tramps upon the roads:[41]
>
>> When I began to inquire,
>> To watch, and question those I met, and speak
>> Without reserve to them, the lonely roads
>> Were open schools, in which I daily read
>> With most delight the passions of mankind,
>> Whether by words, looks, sighs, or tears
>>   revealed;
>> There saw into the depths of human souls,
>> Souls that appear to have no depth at all
>> To careless eyes.

C. S. Lewis, from a slightly different perspective,
makes the same point: 'Next to the Blessed Sacrament itself, your neighbour is the holiest object presented to your senses. If he is a Christian neighbour
he is holy in almost the same way, for in him also
Christ *vere latitat*—the glorifier and the glorified,
Glory Himself is truly hidden.'[42]

It is the contemplative with the 'eye of love' who
best discerns the hidden glory of our humanity,

notably in God's poor, the reflected 'glory of God in the face of Christ' (II Corinthians 4:6), into whose likeness we are being transformed 'from one degree of glory to another' (II Corinthians 3:18). From everything we can glean from the writings of King, as well as from what other contemporaries observed, it is clear that King had this same 'eye of love'—the eye of the contemplative—although from what we have of his writings and sayings, it would seem that he seldom if ever used the more technical terms of 'contemplation' or 'contemplative'.

6

Spirituality and Friendship

New capacities to love, more and more.[1]

It was Saturday, 25 April 1885—St Mark's Day—in St Paul's Cathedral, when Edward King, aged fifty-five (although, as people frequently commented, looking older than his years), was consecrated bishop in the Church of God, by Archbishop Benson, with Canon Henry Parry Liddon as the preacher. After speaking briefly of the nature of the episcopal office as being essentially that of a father in God, Liddon went on at great length to speak in the superlative of King's outstanding previous ministry, with particular reference to his influence as a pastor and teacher:

> Never, probably, in our time has the great grace of sympathy, controlled and directed by a clear sense of the nature and sacredness of revealed truth, achieved so much among so many young men as has been achieved, first at the Theological College of Cuddesdon, and then from the Pastoral Chair at Oxford, as in the case of my dear and honoured friend. He is surrounded at this solemn moment by hundreds who know and feel that to his care and patience, to his skill and courage, to his

faith and spiritual insight, they owe all that is most precious in life.[2]

After elaborating on King's amazing influence 'among so many young men', hundreds of whom were apparently present, Liddon continues by demonstrating how much King's ministry of 'faith and insight' belonged within the larger, extended tradition and witness of the English Church:

> Certainly, if past experience is any guarantee of what is to come, if there be such a thing as continuity of spiritual character and purpose, then we may hope to witness an episcopate which will rank hereafter with those which in point of moral beauty stand highest on the roll of the later English Church – with Andrewes, with Ken, with Wilson, with Hamilton.[3]

THE ENGLISH SCHOOL OF SPIRITUALITY

That continuity of 'spiritual character and purpose' to which Liddon alluded in the persons of Bishops Andrewes, Ken and others, is the continuity traced through the apostolic succession of what can loosely be referred to as the English school of spirituality, which traces its apostolic line back to the eleventh-century archbishop of Canterbury, St Anselm (1033 to 1109).

The guiding lights across the centuries in that distinctive tradition are St Anselm, Julian of Norwich, Margery Kempe of Lynn, the poet-priest George Herbert, John Donne, Nicholas Ferrar of Little

Gidding, and others, among whom, as hopefully will become more evident, we would see Bishop Edward King. For, in so many ways, King can clearly be seen as a classic latter day example of 'the English school' in likewise being 'sane, wise, ancient, modern, sound, and simple; with roots in the New Testament and the Fathers'.[4]

Although there is no evidence that King was consciously aware of belonging to any such school, however loosely defined, nevertheless it is abundantly clear from the notes of his pastoral lectures and from other such writings of his as we have, that whether consciously or unconsciously, such was the tradition of that English 'school' which King both taught his students and exemplified in his own person: it is the unitive character of the English school, and again as with King, its balance and its wholeness. 'Its exponents are eager not to put asunder what God has joined together; head and heart, doctrine and devotion, worship and daily life, dogma and pastoral warmth and love of souls',[5] to which we need to add for the purposes of this particular study, the love of God and the love of neighbour.

As this study of King's spirituality aims to demonstrate, it is precisely this balance and harmony which were at the roots of King's unique influence—an influence, to which Liddon referred, on more than one occasion, as constituting 'nothing less than a form of genius'.

In the so-called English School, there is an 'extraordinary consistency in maintaining the speculative-affective synthesis; the theological and the emotional, doctrine and devotion, fact and feeling'.[6] We see this same harmony in St Anselm as well as in the writings of Julian of Norwich, *Revelations of Divine Love*, all alike so typical of the mystical awakening of the fourteenth century. We can trace this same synthesis of doctrine and devotion in what the Book of Common Prayer holds together in such terms as, 'true piety and sound learning', and all alike belonging to the Benedictine spirituality with its balance of work and prayer, study and worship.

And it's precisely this same harmony that we see in the English school of spirituality that we also find in King and not least with regard to the nature of his inner life, by not putting asunder what God has joined together in the unity of the Spirit, and most notably, for the purposes of this study, the friendship of both God and man. Put another way: 'His teaching married head and heart, devotion and dogma in a quite inimitable manner.'[7]

SPIRITUAL FRIENDSHIP

St Anselm, St Aelred of Rievaulx, William of St Thierry and others came to be seen as the 'new fire' of the Cistercian monastic revival, especially in England, which could not help but encourage and spread the devotion of spiritual friendship. In the writings of William of St Thierry, St Anselm and in particular those of St Aelred in *The Mirror of Charity* and *On*

Spiritual Friendship, human relationships of love
and friendship are held and bound together within
an intimate and loving relationship with God, conceived and experienced as friendship.

Aelred, in particular, draws all this together in his
bold affirmation 'God is Friendship', as did St Richard of Chichester, also in that same English School
who, in his well-known prayer, addresses God as
'Friend and Brother', picking up on Christ's own
insistence that he would no longer call those who
followed him 'servants', but 'friends' (John 15:15).

In the writings of Aelred and others of this school,
there is no reticence about human friendship being
perceived as an appropriate analogy for an intimate
relationship with God. Both St Bernard and William
of St Thierry wrote vividly on spiritual friendship,
notably in their huge number of sermons based on
the erotic love poetry of the Song of Songs in the
Old Testament. They applied that same 'erotic' love
as in the Song of Songs between the Beloved and
the Lover, not only to the 'mystical union between
Christ and his Church', as in the words of St Paul,
but also to that indwelling and union between the
Christian disciple and a personal God who can be
known and loved as a friend.

> It is the assurance of the companionship of a
> Friend always able and willing to guide, check,
> and support us in all dangers; a Friend whose rod
> and staff will still be with us, guiding, protecting,
> even through the valley of the shadow of death;
> a Friend whose constant companionship ought
> to lift up our fallen countenance, and give us,

> even now, on the journey of life, a brightness
> that should witness to those who meet us of the
> reality of the companionship we enjoy—all this
> is no mere language of theoretical theology, or
> excited devotional feeling, but may be the sure
> experience of your daily lives.[8]

There is always the particular danger in any post-
humous investigation into the nature of King's
undoubted, compelling gift of love and friendship:
the temptation to spiritualize and categorize the
nature and various expressions of such intimacy
and love by rigidly applying the Greek differentiation between so-called Platonic friendship (*philia*)
and erotic love (*eros*) and by advocating exclusively
that 'cooler' or, as some might say, more 'spiritual'
brand of which religion so often prefers to speak,
namely, charity (*agape*).

Contrary-wise, however, to the Hebrew mind and
language such neatly labelled and differentiated categories of love must have been either ignored or
overridden by those responsible for making up the
canon of what we call the Old Testament by permit-
ting the inclusion of the Song of Songs. The text of
the Song of Songs makes no apologies for blatantly
being, at one level, an erotic love poem. Yet, throughout history, preachers from widely differing traditions, from the Cistercian St Bernard of the twelfth
century to the Protestant preacher Spurgeon of the
twentieth century, who both alike preached numerous sermons drawing on that erotic love poem, and
not just as an analogy. Rather it is exemplified as a

model, indicative not only of that mystical union between Christ and his Church, but also the intimate union between God in Christ and the Christian disciple, and all as a piece. 'The Song is a mixture of the sensual and the spiritual',[9] both alike drawing us, to quote from King's favourite poet, Dante, to that same 'love that moves the sun and the other stars'. It is the same love that draws and attracts us to God as well as to one another in God.

Following on from this, it would seem that it is not so much the powerful existence of what the Greek mind would speak of as erotic, as the direction and the end to which the unquestionable power of eros and our sexual drive is directed, as well as to what it is harnessed, which gives a strong lead in this whole enquiry into the nature of King's intimate friendships. Augustine gives a helpful analogy, and very much drawn from his own struggles with directing his erotic sexuality to appropriate ends: 'Cleanse your love', he exclaims, but not by sanitizing it or filtering out 'erotic' elements, but rather by 'diverting into the garden the water that was running down the drain',[10] for the nurturing of flowers and the fruit of good works.

Augustine, with whose writings King was well acquainted and whose writings he strongly recommended to his students, struggled for many years with his own powerful sexual drives but found no resolution in the Manichaean teachings, which sought to keep the drive for union of *eros* separate from a purely spiritual love. The breakthrough for him came when he no longer separated out what he calls the 'higher things' from the 'lower things' in a dualistic world view or an idealized view of Christian spirituality.

> I no longer desired a better world, because I was thinking of creation as a whole; and in the light of this more balance discernment, I had come to see that higher things are better than the lower, but that the sum total of all creation is better than the higher things alone.[11]

Philip Seldon, an author from a very different tradition, reiterates the need for joining together what so many throughout the centuries have doggedly kept apart, and all in the name of the sanitized spiritual.

> People have erected a middle wall of partition between two forms of love: the love of God (the New Testament word, *agape*) and passionate human yearning (*eros*—a word never found in the New Testament). I want to argue that these divorced partners need reuniting.[12]

It would seem that in the more affirmative school of English Spirituality as well as in the person and teaching of King, these two were not only reunited but also redirected in much the same way as Augustine suggests, seeking to hold together sacramentally both the sacred and the secular, the holy and the homely, in a 'unitive wholeness', to quote Newton, or as what Augustine termed 'the lower' together with 'the higher'. In that way, the 'lower' (*eros*) is raised, fully incorporated and transposed into a 'higher' key as the 'sum total of all creation', rather than separating out the supposedly 'higher things', or purely spiritual things.

In some remarks at the Cuddesdon Festival in 1900, King clearly felt free to speak very much from the heart of that 'higher life' which he had learned and experienced during his years at Cuddesdon:

> It was at Cuddesdon, that I learned to realize more than ever I did before the possibility of the reality of the love of God and the love of man. Somehow the cloud of conventionality which hangs over us so constantly seemed to be lifted off, and we saw something more into the hearts and lives of others.[13]

In the last sermon King preached at Christ Church before leaving Oxford for Lincoln in 1885, he spells out and applies this same Augustinian formula with telling clarity: 'By God's great goodness we Christians can look up higher than our own nature, for we have seen His nature descend, not to destroy, but to take up humanity into the Godhead.'[14]

And as on another occasion previously, when again he refers to the lessons he learned in his years at Cuddesdon:

> It was here that I learned to realize more than I ever did before, the possibility of the reality of the love of God and the love of man . . . My life [in Cuddesdon] gave me hope of a higher life for myself, and a higher life for other people too.[15]

'A higher life for himself' and 'a higher life for other people' — to what is that a subtle and understated reference? Later he refers again to this even more explicitly when addressing his former students from Cuddesdon, after his consecration as bishop in St Paul's in 1885. On that occasion, referring back to those years at Cuddesdon he spoke of being 'brought to love God, and one another in God, in a real and special way, not understood by people unless they themselves knew what it was to be thus free'.[16]

Surely it is that precious gift of friendship, as experienced just as powerfully as falling in love as in courtship leading to the union of marriage—a covenanted relationship reflecting that unconditional love and acceptance as in the covenant and mystical union betwixt Christ and his Church. Was it during his time at Cuddesdon that King experienced some kind of further awakening and self-discovery?

THE RECONCILIATION OF APPARENT OPPOSITES

> It is the great work of God to bring man back again to himself, and into loving communion with his fellow men. This is the work at which our Saviour tells us his Father worked hitherto, and he worked.
>
> It is our great privilege, yours and mine, to share in this work of reconciliation, so that in God, man may find that fullness of rest which apart from him, he cannot find— rest of mind in knowing the truth, rest of the heart in coming nearer to the personal God in knowledge and love.

And then the old familiar core of gospel ministry as

practised throughout the years of his previous ministry, and which was to be reiterated both in words
and actions throughout the next twenty-five years:
all that, so 'that in Christ we may all draw nearer to
God and to each other'.[17]

In that way, as Aquinas insisted, Grace serves to
perfect what is natural rather than destroying, sub-
limating or suppressing it, in some misguided quest
for a wrongly perceived and idealized perfectionism
in the pursuit of some more refined 'spirituality'. In
the classic aphorism of von Hügel, 'Grace is not the
cuckoo which drives all other birds out of the nest',
or put another way, not by driving out what many
wrongly perceive as the ugly duckling of *eros* in order
to make exclusive room for a supposedly 'higher'
and more 'spiritual' breed!

In all of this, we must surely sense that we are now
approaching 'King territory' with the landscape, or
as Gerard Manley Hopkins might say, the 'inscape' of
King's spiritualty and inner life, most conspicuously
evident in and expressed through his intimate and
formative friendships.

'GOD IS FRIENDSHIP'

What is abundantly clear is that it demonstrably was
the experience of King's own daily life which to a
large measure accounts for his attractive influence
with all whom he met. Furthermore, it would seem
for King, as was said of Aelred, that there was 'no

conflict between love of our friends and the love of God, since all love is one, albeit differently expressed and has its source in God. The love of neighbour is no derogation of our love of God, but rather is necessary for us if we are truly to love him. It is this identification of spiritual friendship with the perfect love of God which allowed Aelred to suggest the phrase, 'God is friendship'.

'The theme of friendship held an important place in the thought of the ancient world and the Middle Ages; from Cicero and Cassian, to Bernard and Aelred, the ideal of the union of the souls of good men in the pursuit of virtue grew and achieved a place in Christian theology'—and not least in the theology of Anselm and in his 'Prayer for his Friends'.[18]

'It is the love that God in Christ has for men that interests [Anselm], and it is from this that he draws his love for other men. Christ is "the good friend" and it is in that friendship that men find fellowship with each other.'

But Anselm goes further yet:

'Yet within this love, Anselm recognizes quite simply that there are some whom Christ's love has impressed on his heart "with a special and more intimate love", and so he prays specially for them'[19] in his *Prayer for his Friends.*

So by relating human friendship closely with God's friendship for his friends, Anselm, and especially Aelred, 'avoided the problem of defining its moral limits', or being 'troubled by the twentieth century's pervasive consciousness of sexual drives', or by feeling 'obliged to discuss sexual pathology in a treatise on spiritual friendship'.[20]

Biographers of Aelred readily point out that the close and very emotional friendships which Aelred, later in life, was free to enjoy as abbot in the monastery, prove that a negative reaction to his own youthful crush on a male member of the court in Scotland before he entered the monastery, 'did not inhibit his emotional freedom in later life. It is also interesting to remember that Walter Daniel [his contemporary biographer] specifically noted that Aelred, unlike some other abbots, was not scandalised by demonstrations of affection such as holding hands, by the monks'. Aelred, in other words, seems to have had not only 'confidence in his own ability to deal with the sexual component of his friendships, but to have trusted his monks to be able to do the same. Nor is there any evidence that Aelred's confidence was misjudged.'[21]

Perhaps at this point we are getting somewhere near to unravelling the secret of that 'genius' of which Liddon spoke and which Scott Holland, from experience of his long-standing close friendship with King, endorses with his customary, and admittedly euphoric eloquence:

> His natural manhood always found itself, in whatever he did: and showed itself complete and distinctive. And Grace had so intimately mingled with his nature that it was all of one piece. Grace itself had become natural. Who could say which was which? Was it all Grace? Was it all nature? Was it not all both? Anyhow,

> the whole man moved altogether, in every word
> and act. There were no separate compartments;
> and no disturbing reserves . . . so that the impact
> that he made upon one was absolutely simple
> and undivided. The central spirit tingled in
> every pressure of the hand, in every turn of the
> voice, in every gleam of the eye. You had the
> whole of him, whenever you touched him. That
> was one of the delights of his companionship.[22]

So yes, indeed, 'the whole man moved together', so
that 'you had the whole of him'; 'everything hung
together'. Is that perhaps what the adjective 'holy'
or 'whole' is striving to communicate when speaking
of those whom the Church delights to recognize as
saints? It is that same wholeness and integration of
King's person to which Owen Chadwick, from his
extensive research, also testifies, saying that King
made people feel that the Christian life 'was supernatural, yes; otherworldly, yes; but not strange, or
unnatural, or forced, or inhuman, or narrow. This
was what man was born for. It was normality itself.
It was balanced, sane, unwarped. It was man as he
ought to be.'[23]

Perhaps it was something of that balanced and
proportionate sense which that young carpenter
sought to embody in a beautifully proportioned
wooden box which he gave to King when he left
Wheatley. King kept the little leaving present in his
study throughout his entire life and was always
delighted to show it to visitors, quoting as he did
so often the words of the donor: 'I knew you would
like it, sir, because it is the same on each side.'[24] It was

an exact square, perfectly proportioned, re-imaging presumably through his craft what the young man had perceived and experienced in the person of King during his curacy in Wheatley.

It would seem that as his life and ministry developed King achieved this balance, this synthesis, this wholeness or, as what others who knew him well came to recognize, that 'radiant and attractive holiness', to which Scott Holland so powerfully testified.

In words, rather than wood, Owen Chadwick re-affirms what that young man had observed of King's person: 'One of the secrets of his later power, was the naturalness of his faith. Faith was nothing strange in the world. The love of God was never fanatical or irrational'. King always conveyed 'a perfect harmony between nature and grace'.[25]

We also have further evidence of this unitive wholeness from the lips of King himself when, in 1885 he addressed a gathering of former Cuddesdon students, in his characteristically understated, subtle and highly sensitive way, in the chapter house of St Paul's Cathedral, after his consecration as bishop of Lincoln:

> At Cuddesdon, we wished to offer up our life and be happy, blessed in ourselves, and with the privilege of giving that blessedness to others . . . Cuddesdon drew us nearer to God and to one another; giving us the peculiar freedom and elasticity which made us so loose and free (though not wild) in head and heart . . . Our hearts were surrendered to be disentangled and disciplined, to find their rest when given

up to God . . . We were brought to love God, and one another in God, in a real and special way, not understood by people unless they themselves knew what it is to be thus free . . . All grows really clear by taking God for our rest and end, with a sense of the reality of love and need of discipline. It gives a wonderful power of expansion as the love of God and man is proved as a rule of life.[26]

Of course such remarks are wildly open to misinterpretation: that freedom and elasticity which made them 'loose and free in head and heart' clearly was not understood by many then, any more than it ever has been, or, as King said, 'by people, unless they themselves knew what it is to be thus free'; and all that giving 'a wonderful power of expansion as the love of God and man is proved' (perhaps validated) 'in a rule of life' — a whole new and integrated way of life.

There is certainly nothing suppressed in all of that, and yet it speaks also of the need for hearts to be disentangled and disciplined, not as an end in itself but rather in order to achieve greater freedom. In spiritual direction there is generally the suggestion of a suitable rule of life as it was termed and still is. It would seem that such was the kind of rule of life by which King himself lived and which he commended to others, and all that in a quest for a holy freedom, resulting from discipline and self-restraint, best summarized in that enigmatic and paradoxical aphorism of Augustine which King mentioned in his *Pastoral Lectures*: 'Love God and do as you like'.

FREEDOM AND DISCIPLINE

Before concluding with such affirming optimism, it is vitally important not to overlook the place of discipline and self-restraint which certainly held a firm place in King's teaching, as well as in his own intimate and influential friendships. In all intimate relationships, whether of marriage, partnerships or friendships, there must always be a place for boundaries which respect the personal integrity of the other.

> As with God's relationships with us, human intimacy involves holding in proper balance an appropriate dissolution of personal boundaries and yet the continued respect for personal space. It is an unfortunate fact, of which we are being made increasingly aware these days, that the sexual crossing of boundaries has often been violent and abusive. At the heart of most cases of sexual abuse, including rape, lies the desire to gain power over another human being. Sexual violation of boundaries seems to be used to meet a number of needs that have little to do with real sexual desires, let alone with love. True human desire, just like God's desire for us, is respectfully attuned both to the self and to the partner. Each person may be lost in the other but individual boundaries are not abused or invaded. Each person allows them to be crossed in a way that enhances each partner rather than destroys his or her identity.[27]

Although King was optimistic about human nature, in a way so characteristic of the English school of spirituality, he was not naïve: for all his warmth and loving pastoral affection, as one who knew King well readily testified, 'you felt that he had himself well in hand, that he had disciplined that strong affectionate heart and that burning zeal, and this discipline showed itself in self-restraint and gentleness'.[28]

'King was unmarried, and it must have been a great temptation for so naturally affectionate a man to seek relief from loneliness in the society and friendship of the young. He knew, however, that for their sakes his feelings had to be disciplined in order to leave him free to love *all* with the love of Christ. What this cost him emerges in advice which he gave to a tutor in a missionary college'[29] who was experiencing great difficulty in 'getting through' to the students of very differing cultures to achieve any sense of collegiate community even vaguely resembling the community at Cuddesdon under King.

> It will want *heaps* of *talk* — MOUNTAINS of talk — with individuals, and you will have to be worn out and out, and done for, and broken-hearted, and miserable, and not understood, and deceived, before you begin to get the right sort of relationship which is absolutely necessary for the students' sake *now* . . . and get them to see that you are heart and soul in earnest to bring them one and all, not to yourself but to the mind of Christ.

And again, he says:

> Only by breaking your poor heart in pieces over and over again can you hope to make them begin to think of believing that there is such

a thing as love! Don't mind, be miserable, but don't stop loving them . . . I can only say you will never regret *all* the misery you go through.[30]

Something of those letters, written in 1880 and 1882, reveals the measure and cost of such a love and care for others, as well as the self-discipline required by any who would seek to influence for good those in their care. B. W. Randolph, who was a student of King at Oxford, and later became principal of Ely Theological College, clearly witnessed at first hand the importance of that same self-discipline in King's pastoral ministry in Oxford: 'Above all he had a deep and disciplined affection for young men, and especially for the young men with whom he had to do at the Theological College . . . This power of disciplined affection was one of the highest qualifications for his work.'[31]

Yet, this strong self-discipline in King should never be mistaken for self-flagellation, a practice which would have been totally out of character with him. There is clear evidence however that the practice of self-flagellation, the scourge or the 'discipline' as it was known, was used among some Tractarians with whom Gladstone had some association. 'The idea of its use for what was intended as a punishment for sin probably came to Gladstone in a Tractarian context. Newman certainly used a scourge and described it in his novel, *Loss and Gain*, as "an iron discipline or scourge, studded with nails". Pusey asked Gladstone's closest friend, James Hope, to bring him a "discipline" from the continent, and hoped that Keble, his confessor, would advise him to use it.'[32]

King's self-discipline which he advocated for his ordinands, as well as practised himself, was, as he frequently pointed out, always for the sake of those whom pastors and priests are called to serve. In his *Pastoral Lectures* he specifically warned his students to be alert and to practise vigilance in this matter: 'Let him that thinketh he standeth take heed.' He urges the need for moral purity and self-control, but always and notably for the sake of security and peace and freedom. Those who are ordained will have to offer spiritual guidance to others and must 'see the way' themselves. Supremely, 'because we must follow Christ. At least let us be pure for the sake of others. He could be in public places and elsewhere. Alone with women of infamous character because holy, guileless, undefiled, separate . . . "For their sakes I sanctify myself." We want priests who can go without scandal into Sodom, and draw men out.'[33]

In those same *Pastoral Lectures*, he spells out the need to be alert to self-deception, speaking of 'little acts of affection' as being 'often the preludes to sin. Love we must, but so as to be in heaven together'. And again, 'Lust is the very essence of selfishness'.[34]

It is clear that for King, discipline was always a means to an end and not an end in itself, and neither was it the quest for perfectionism in any form. This is vividly exemplified in one of his many spiritual letters of guidance and advice, in which he makes it clear that the discipline which he is commending is really a 'pruning' as in Christ's own teaching, and all for the sake of a more abundant fruitfulness, a more extended loving, not less (John 15:2). King's letter is a reply to an earlier letter from an ordinand who had enjoyed a very close friendship with 'H', with whom he lived. However, in order for H to carry out his father's wishes there would now need to be a parting of the ways, when the ordinand would need to return to his home in Wantage, feeling, as King says, 'a little silently sad', and without his friend. Clearly the ordinand, possibly one of King's former students at Oxford, must have known Professor King well enough to have felt sufficiently confident to confide something so intimate to him and, furthermore that King, with his customary sympathy and compassion would understand something of his pain and sadness, which, in what we have of King's reply, it would seem that he most certainly did.

> I should have written last night, because I felt you must be a little silently sad. But, dearest child, it will be all right. The more we can throw our wills in with the great Will of God . . . the stronger our lives become; so it is much better that H. should carry out his father's wish, and that you should give up, rather than break off, and begin on you own independent wills. And then, do let me reassure you that the heart is of such immense capacity if we only give it up to God to discipline, that these woundings are rather *prunings* for greater beauty and richer fruit. Had you gone with your good friend it might have narrowed the circle of your love, and you would not have had the sense of freedom

> to love all who may be waiting to be won by
> you to Him through your real love of them.
> *Now* there is a sense of solitude, of sadness, but
> believe me, that will be more, *infinitely more*,
> than filled by that which is to come. These acts
> of divine discipline are simply invitations to
> trust our hearts to *Him*.

King is clearly here encouraging and pastoring what
might be termed a 'special friendship' and at the
same time helping to set it within the call of pastoral ministry which calls for discipline within the
'greater circle of love', as he puts it, given by God
to those who are called to bring others to a knowledge of God's greater love. In doing this 'you will
be helping another soul to realize what he believes
but does not quite feel, the *unity of all in Christ*, and
all the while your greater love for God will give you
new capacities and power to love more and more'.[35]

Henry Nouwen makes this same point even more
pointedly, when writing about the close, intimate
friendship which existed between Jane de Chantal
and Francis de Sales, in what Nouwen calls 'a Jesus-
centred, affectionate friendship'. Such a relationship
allows plenty of space and freedom to both parties,
while being open enough for a wider, loving ministry to others, as King advised in his letter to the
young man.

> Francis and Jane are two people whose friendship
> is solidly anchored in their common love of God.
> They are not two lonely people who cling to each
> other in order to find a safe home, in the midst
> of a fearful world. Both of them have found

Jesus as the bridegroom of their souls. He is the fulfillment of all their desires. Without Jesus, friends tend to become possessive of each other and are easily tempted to violence when mutual expectations are not fulfilled. With Jesus there remains ample freedom for the unique ways of the individual persons. Without Jesus, friends tend to close in on each other, and ignore the larger world. With Jesus friendships can bear fruit which many can enjoy.[36]

Clearly, in speaking of what Nouwen calls a 'Jesus-centred friendship, King is speaking from the heart of his own experience and not from some textbook on pastoral theology. Such words powerfully witness to how he had found for himself, through God's discipline and 'pruning' that 'yet more excellent way' to the 'greater love for God' with, as in that letter, 'new capacities and power to love, more and more'.

It was something of those 'new capacities and power to love' which undoubtedly resourced King's amazing and transformative influence throughout the whole of his life and ministry at Cuddesdon, Oxford and Lincoln as being, in those words of Liddon, previously quoted, 'nothing less than a form of genius'.

7

King as Soul Friend and Spiritual Counsellor

We truly educate when we educe, draw out, unfold, perfect that common humanity which is in every man wherever and whatever he may be.[1]

PASTORAL THEOLOGY AND THE MINISTRY OF SPIRITUAL DIRECTION

'Spiritual direction is itself central to the English School of Spirituality, not only as pastoral practice, but also as the source and inspiration of pastoral and ascetical theology.'[2] However, to the mind of the English school of spirituality, the phrase 'spiritual direction' acquires rather too much of an authoritarian, Counter-Reformation taint. 'Soul Friend' or 'Fellow Traveller', or even the Gaelic word *anam cara* from the Celtic tradition describes more accurately the role of the spiritual guide, as opposed to the language which would speak of 'spiritual direction' or a 'spiritual director', and is so much more in keeping with the tone of the pastoral oversight of the English school of spirituality with its preferred nomenclature of 'spiritual guide' or 'soul friend'. Such is precisely what Alastair Campbell suggests in his *Rediscovering Pastoral Care*:

> 'Teachers must be *companions* on the same journey that we ourselves are making. Their authority derives from their ability to be fellow travellers, friends and comrades on this journey ... Teaching thus defined, is in essence a transaction between persons; teaching in the form of *exploration* endeavours to evoke a questioning and searching response in the learner. This is done by communicating something of the teacher's own struggle to understand, his own need to be a learner as well as a teacher.[3]

By whatever name, it was supremely as a spiritual guide and mentor that King was best able in those early years as principal at Cuddesdon to develop his unique gift for moulding the common life of the Cuddesdon community, as well as by directing the souls and forwarding the vocation of individual members of the College. Over the subsequent years as professor of pastoral theology at Oxford and as bishop of Lincoln, that particular skill in ministry became increasingly sought after by a large number of men and women for whom King became a formative mentor and soul friend.

It was the same with regard to his pastoralia lectures in which he gives a theological foundation for the practice and ministry of pastoral care and spiritual direction, constantly particularizing the role of the pastor as being primarily that of a physician of the soul, commissioned and spiritually empowered for the ministry of the cure of souls.

King drew from a large range of authors and indeed of traditions to inform both his lectures on pastoral theology as well as his practice as a spiritual counsellor concerned with spiritual formation. Although King made frequent references to Richard Baxter's *The Reformed Pastor*, yet here again, as with his lectures on preaching or teaching in general, with King there is always less of an exhortatory, didactic tone and more of a call to the inner life of the Spirit, always characteristically ministered with sympathy, compassion and something of the human touch, or as we might say in the case of physicians, even with something of 'the bedside manner'. Baxter lists dogmatically seven pastoral functions, shades of which, albeit in a lighter tone, are also traceable in King's teaching and practice: conversion of the unconverted; advice to enquirers; building up the already converted; oversight of families in the congregation; visiting the sick; reproof of the impenitent; exercise of discipline.

Although King always encouraged his students to read Baxter, yet for much of his 'hands-on' practice of pastoral care and spiritual counselling, King unashamedly drew deeply from a rather different source, from the European mind, and in particular from the prodigious writings of Bishop Johann Michael Sailer of Regensburg, formally and for many years, like King, a professor of pastoral theology. Both King and Sailer were conspicuous in bringing to their work as professors in a university context a radically different approach to our understanding of both theology and pastoral care—a difference which the Church today would do well to revisit.

Bishop Talbot, writing in particular of King's pastoralia lectures during his time at Oxford, recalls:

> I remember how he talked of the big work on Pastoral Theology, by Bishop Sailer, at which he had worked hard, and his [Sailer's] was a pastoral chair; and in that line of teaching, he [King] was inimitable, so human, so sagacious, so penetrating, so devout. The spell was felt at once. His class rolled up to unprecedented figures, and hundreds of young candidates for Holy Orders went out from Oxford carrying with them not only such and such convictions which he had helped to form in his interpretation of Hooker, but even more with his thoughts and hints about dealing with their flocks of which they must have felt the touch most in the least controversial and most practical parts of their work. It was the old influence of the Cuddesdon Parochialia deepened and widened.[4]

Unquestionably, it would have been in those same lectures that King would have been most at home, not only drawing from his time and experience at Cuddesdon as vicar, but also as a teacher in his capacity as principal.

'One felt all the time', wrote one graduate who had stayed on at Oxford to read for Holy Orders and who had attended assiduously King's lectures, 'that one was in the presence of a master, but at the same time of one whose conception of the Pastoral Office was the outcome not merely of wide reading, but of profound conviction based on personal experience.'[5]

For those same pastoralia lectures, in addition to Sailer, King drew on a huge range of writers from a broad range of traditions; from the early fathers and the Schoolmen, to St Gregory's classic treatment in his *Pastoral Care;* from St Bernard of Clairvaux and St Augustine's *Confessions* as well as *De Doctrina Christiana Book IV*, especially for homiletics; St Chrysostom, St Basil and St Bonaventura and by no means least from the writings of Francis de Sales—in particular *The Introduction to the Devout Life.* In his teaching on scripture and the Book of Common Prayer he drew on a cross section of Anglican Divines: Hooker, Andrewes, Jeremy Taylor, Bishop Bull, all laced with frequent quotations from the great Tractarians, whose disciple he openly confessed himself to be: Newman, Pusey, Keble, Marriott, Liddon, Mason Neale. Yet, at the same time he found fruitful matter for training in pastoral understanding in the works of Juvenal, Suetonius and Aristotle. By any measure, it is an impressively broad range of resources.

Although in the published notes of the lectures there is little specific reference to the influence of Bishop Sailer's three volumes on pastoral theology, to which from other sources we know that King in practice made frequent reference, yet it was from the blend of an applied theology of pastoral care derived from a lifetime's experience that a whole generation of clergy were given a new vitality and skill to equip them in their future ministry, and not least in this particular skill of spiritual direction and Christian formation.

> The lively presentation, the wealth of source material—these were important; but even more, King's lectures drew men because they mediated his profound sympathy with all sorts and conditions of men. It is the same sympathy we find in his letters and sermons, and in all his pastoral dealings. The width of his sympathy determines the breadth of his reading, so that we can say of the *Pastoral Lectures* . . . that all human life is there.[6]

KING'S DISTINCTIVE TOUCH

Both in his teaching and preaching, everything was further informed from King's knowledge of the human heart and the narrative of human life, to which be brought his own distinctive and characteristic lightness of touch. The need for a 'light touch' in pastoral care and ministry were beautifully and memorably illustrated on the occasion of King's first return to Oxford after his consecration as bishop. In the course of the speech he gave on that occasion, he refers to the cleaning out of his study at Christ Church, in preparation for his move to Lincoln. By the end of the day of his move, the only single remaining object was a match box: printed on it were just two words which summarized and yet which spoke volumes of the nature of King's pastoral care and oversight: 'rub lightly':[7]

'It was a marvellous speech,' commented Father J. G. Adderley, the founder of Oxford House, in the East End of London, who was present to hear King. 'We were to rub the East Enders—that is, we were to be definite, firm, sane, judicious; but we were to do it 'lightly', with love and sympathy. We were not to use too much of the ecclesiastical 'must'; but 'just take them and give them a little push—no more.' The speech literally took us all by storm.[8]

This begins to give something of the measure of King's transforming influence, which sought neither to control, to clone or to override, but rather to enable a trustful outpouring and confiding which is only possible in a non-threatening and secure relationship. In a lengthy letter, the Rev'd J. E. Swallow, who had been a student at Cuddesdon during King's time as principal, attempted to set out something of what the impact of King's ministry there had been:

Until now we had never understood ourselves. At last the tangle was unraveled by one as familiar, it seemed, with every twist and turn as if he himself had lived it out along with us. Doctrine, sermon, meditation each went home with direct personal application, until it was plain that our only course was to submit our lives and difficulties, our temptations and our sins, our hopes and fears to one who seemed to know them all without needing to be told, and so benefit by the guidance for the future from one who had shown himself clairvoyant of the past.[9]

The fragment of a spiritual letter from King to an unknown recipient reflects this same quiet confidence in self-worth and affirmation.

'While at Oxford as an undergraduate (1874–1877)', wrote a student who was subsequently ordained, 'I attended three courses of Dr King's lectures at Christ Church. At the last lecture of his, which I was privileged to attend, at the end of the Summer Term, 1877, he gave his students what I then thought, and still think, very sound advice, which ran somewhat as follows—"Avoid, if possible, rushing straight from the University into Holy Orders. Seek rather to learn as much as you can of human nature, by mixing with men and women, studying their characters, and learning their needs. Travel, if you can; and, if need be, work at any honourable calling to support yourselves, until you have learned to reach the hearts of men and women."'[10]

A student who was not an ordinand tells of how King's official lectures as professor of pastoral theology, although mainly addressed to those who were going on to be ordained, nevertheless drew many others to the private lectures he gave at his home in Christ Church:

> His power of sympathy amounted to genius, and gave him an almost supernatural insight into human hearts. He spoke to us of our past lives, of our future prospects, of our present temptations, of our besetting sins, with an intimate penetration engendered by long experience in personal contact with souls. He

told us truths about ourselves which were part of our consciousness, but which we believed to have been hidden from all except ourselves.[11]

The fragment of a Spiritual Letter from King to Charlie, a lad from King's Wheatley days, who had gone to Culham to train as a teacher, reflects King's consistent, quiet self-confidence in having a right self-acceptance as the first step to becoming who God created us to be, as in the words of the *Jubilate*: 'It is he that hath made us and not we ourselves.' So, he writes:

> Just throw yourself back on the fact that God made you what you are, and, therefore, do not fear failure or want of power.[12]

It was precisely this sensitivity and the knowledge of the inner workings of human nature, learned mainly in the school of experience, in which King excelled and which he clearly saw as necessarily being so central to every aspect of a pastoral ministry worthy of the name: the kind of knowledge which can be lost in the pursuit of a knowledge derived principally if not exclusively and 'second-hand', so to speak, from books and the intellect, a common failing in the world of academia. As for the need of such a 'knowledge' of human nature, King, here as elsewhere, is consistently forthright:

> Unless you understand human nature you will not be a good preacher, though you may be a great theologian. This knowledge of human nature must exist in order to apply the other

> knowledge. You may also learn much by a
> knowledge of yourself, but you must get hold
> of human nature *somehow.*[13]

As with Christ himself, it could have been said of King that 'He knew all men and needed no one to bear witness of man; for he himself knew what was in man' (John 2:25).

Allied to that knowledge of the heart was 'a sanctified common sense' as perfectly exemplified in some advice which King gave to one of his ordinands in 1873. The man had scruples about going on a shooting expedition during the vacation: King readily advises him to go ahead and shoot.

> I am not saying all this out of false kindness
> . . . but because I do value so highly a natural
> growth in holiness, a humble grateful accep-
> tance of the circumstances God has provided
> for each of us, and I dread the unnatural,
> forced, cramped ecclesiastical holiness, which
> is so much more quickly produced, but is so
> human and so poor.[14]

There is another delightful incident during King's years as principal of Cuddesdon, which is so illustrative of his aversion to a self-conscious striving for an unnatural, self-styled piety—'forced' and 'cramped'. 'To one student on Good Friday, who had eaten very little during the days of Holy Week, he gave the following advice: "Dearest man, eat breakfast and come down to the level of Yours, E.K."'[15] So, the heart for King was not only and always the heart of the matter, whatever that matter might be, but rather and more poignantly, it was to the hearts of pupils and friends alike that King, as teacher, mentor and soul friend aimed to reach and to motivate towards to an ever-closer relationship with, and participation in, the life of the Spirit, the source of true and authentic holiness. Indeed, it could be said of King, as of the great saint, the Abbé Huvelin, who reportedly much preferred to 'write in souls'; to draw out, perfect, and unfold, 'that common humanity which is in every man', and to do it, whether in the reading of books or the reading of souls, to do everything 'by the light of Christ'.

So, by the same 'light of Christ', King urged his students: 'Read the poets ethically—e.g., Aeschylus, Dante, Homer, Shakespeare, Milton, Tennyson. Read good sermons, such as Newman's. Read thoughtfully: analyze them.' He especially urged them to 'read good novels. You will thus travel into circumstances, and conditions, and situations of life.'

'Thy gentleness', or as in the Coverdale translation, 'thy loving correction hath made me great', from Psalm 18:35, was one of King's favourite texts, although there was nothing weak or sentimental about such gentleness. True gentleness of spirit, in practice is restrained, even disciplined strength rightly directed, never in order to put down, but contrary-wise, always to encourage, to build up and raise up. King is often seen, in this and in other respects as an Anglican version of St Francis de Sales who wrote, 'Nothing is so strong as gentleness— nothing so loving and gentle as strength'.[16]

'AN ELECTRIC ARK OF INFLUENCE'

What was said of the Tractarians generally could equally well be said of King and of the nature of his influence, that 'while in their priestly offices and personal lives they remained distrustful of display, the almost magnetic energy produced by so much passionate intensity held under control by a restraining simplicity of life was a source of powerful attraction. To many who gathered about them it made them appear to glow with an inner light. They seemed to make the unseen world real. They stood close to the holy God.'[17]

One such mentor of King, who had undoubtedly 'stood close to the holy God', was the Rev'd John Day. John Day had tutored and mentored King as a boy of sixteen in preparation for going up to Oxford, and had had a huge formative influence on the young King, not only for his studies but also for his spiritual formation in those early formative years. Returning to Ellesmere in 1879, for the occasion of laying the foundation stone of the St Oswald's College, later to be known as Ellesmere College, in a speech Professor King, as he was by then, paid a huge tribute to his former tutor and mentor and in the course of the speech spoke of Day as being 'An Electric Ark of Personal Influence'.[18] In truth, nothing less could equally be said of King himself throughout the whole of his ministry.

Wherever he went and with whoever he met, King had an enormous formative influence to 'draw them to Christ' and not least to the ordained ministry of his Church; an influence which Archbishop Tait lamented as being singularly lacking in Oxford where, from his perspective, it was most needed. Writing in his diary on 4 January 1880, he records a 'most interesting talk he had had' with a friend on 'the religious state of Oxford'.

> It would seem, that there are numbers of young men who would easily be influenced to give themselves to the clerical life if any man of real power of influencing them, like Arnold, were to appear there as a teacher. The only person with power of influencing in this way is King, but his theological opinions do not perhaps attract the more intelligent . . . young men who might be led right' but who 'sink into a sort of Agnosticism or indifference from the mere want of powerful guidance.

Tait concludes by affirming that 'the right man would spring up some day, and that in a University, as shown in the case of Newman, it is wonderful how one man with great powers can affect a whole generation'.[19] Yet, for those with eyes to see, King had clearly done just that, yet not so much with the great power of intellect, as with the accompanying power of the Spirit and in holiness of life, resulting in a whole generation of men who went on, many of them, either in teaching posts, as parish priests and as bishops, to renew and re-invigorate the ministry and witness of Church for many years to come.

Yet, King's undoubted formative influence had nothing to do with any attempt to control, and least of all to clone. Nothing could have been further from his distinctive way of teaching or mentoring, whether as a spiritual guide or, less formally, as a friend and fellow traveller. Talbot records how when he was preparing to go to Keble College as the first Warden of the newly founded Oxford College, he talked with King about his ideas for the new work as well as about the kind of influence as Warden that he would be able to exert over the students. He records how King cautioned him to avoid the temptation to clone: 'He gave me the wise counsel, "Don't try to Talbotize your men."'[20]

The Franciscan writer and teacher Richard Rohr cautions similarly:

> A spiritual leader who lacks human compassion has almost no power to change other people, because people intuitively know he or she does not represent the Whole or the Holy One. Such leaders need to rely upon rules, laws, costume and enforcement powers to effect any change in others. Such change does not go deep, nor does it last. In fact, it is not really change at all. It is mere conformity.[21]

'True spiritual leaders lead not from above and not even from below, but mostly from *within*, by walking *with* their brothers and sisters, or "smelling like the sheep", as Pope Francis puts it.'[22]

BETHEL

During his time as professor in Oxford and in addition to his lectures and preaching as a canon of Christ Church, together with his work as a recognized spiritual counsellor, King took the opportunity to convert the washhouse in the garden behind his home in Tom Quad, into a little chapel which he named—*Bethel*. It was there, during Term time, where he was able to be much more himself in his Friday evening addresses, uninhibited by the formality of the pulpit of the University Church. In Bethel the talks were more along the lines of informal retreat addresses, of which King became an exponent without equal in later life.

It is in the several reports of those addresses that we catch a glimpse of the breadth of King's appeal, for the men who came to listen were, it seems, 'not a pietistic remnant, pale young curates in the making. They were a good cross-section of the young, mainly undergraduates and included plenty of rowing men. In fact the hearties as well as the aesthetes, the tough and the tender, the clever and the simple, all came to King. When he left Oxford for Lincoln, over three hundred BAs and undergraduates joined together to present him with his episcopal ring, in thanks for all the spiritual help and guidance he had given them, especially through his "Bethel" addresses.'[23]

One such former student tells us:

> The place was full before the appointed time
> to begin and when 'Tom' struck nine—one

can feel again, after so many years—the hush
of expectation, then the opening of the door,
followed by the heavy tread, and, finally, the
sight of the well-known figure, as King, robed
in a very ample and somewhat crumpled
surplice, made his way up the room and knelt
down at the faldstool; there was a pause, then
a Collect, followed by a hymn (sung kneeling),
accompanied by a harmonium; then a prayer,
after which he would stand up and speak as he
alone could speak . . . What we all felt was that
here was a heart beating in sympathy with my
heart; it would help me if I could talk to him;
and he wants me to live close to God so that I
may bring others to God; for that was always his
point of view. He knew that many—probably
the majority—of those to whom he spoke would
be looking forward to Ordination, and he would
often say, 'I am speaking, dear friends, to you
like this for the sake of the poor people to whom
you will, please God, be going.[24]

King's contribution, so evident from the earliest years
of his ministry to the end, was at a personal level, not
only with his pupils and friends, but also with those
who sought him out as a formative pastor. Pastor
and prophet seldom make for good and easy bed
fellows. It seems that what King might have written
in any large, scholarly book, he preferred to write on
the hearts of those whose lives in turn would have
a continuing influence for good, as in a ripple-effect
for future generations of clergy and laity alike and
for many years to come.

Dr Talbot, a much younger don whose time in
Oxford overlapped with that of King, is adamant

that King's influence, far from being limited to the undergraduates, was equally powerful amongst the younger dons:

> His temperament radiated sympathy, mental as well as moral and personal. He felt with men, he felt with his time, he was conscious of the movement under his feet. It did not carry him away, but there was appeal in it; he felt the appeal and responded to it. He wanted to learn as well as to guide; and I feel sure, looking back, that as he got an increasing position he felt drawn to give younger men the sympathy and help which can be given by one who, standing between generations, can feel something of the new as well as the old . . .
>
> Thus it was that both in his personality and in his teaching there was a blend of the strong austerity of the generation behind, and of the more expansive, lighter-hearted (and in many of us shallower-hearted) tone of the generation into which he lived on.[25]

CONFESSOR AND CONFESSION

Increasingly, over the years, King was greatly sought after as a retreat conductor, and then as now, in the course of conducting retreats, an opportunity would usually be given for those who were attending the retreat to spend a little time, one-to-one, with the priest leading the retreat. Frequently, although not always, the interview would lead to the use of the Sacrament of Penance when retreatants would have the opportunity for making their confession.

When King became principal of Cuddesdon in 1863 he had never been to Confession himself, and at that time there was nothing unusual even for High Church Anglicans about that. However, when one of his students asked King to hear his confession, the request brought the whole matter to a head: 'Wait a while,' King told the student, 'I must make my own first.'[26] Shortly afterwards he rode into Oxford to see Dr Pusey to make his Confession, which marked the beginning of his lifelong practice of regular, though not over-frequent use of the Sacrament.

Although he became a noted and much sought-after confessor at Oxford and later at Lincoln, that was never a role he himself sought: he was simply drawn to the practice of it as pastoral need required. As in other aspects of his ministry, he continued to practise a more 'bespoke' rather than an 'off-the-peg' approach both in his practice as a confessor as well as in his teaching about Confession, and all that at a time during the days of the Catholic revival in the Church of England, when the whole matter of the Confessional became such a vexed issue.

King was never an undiscriminating advocate of the confessional, although he openly and indeed from his earliest days courageously defended its healing power as a means of Grace. His mature judgement was that 'it would not be amiss if some of the people who use Confession very frequently would go less often; while he wished that many who never went to Confession, would do so now and then'.

His words to one who had known him for many years were:

> Don't you think dear friend, that it would be a
> good thing if some people did not go *quite* so
> often as they do, and if some who do not go at
> all would go sometimes.[27]

His practice as a confessor, as in so many other respects, combined strength with tenderness, although in some of his letters of spiritual counsel there is sufficient evidence of just how stern he could be when confronted by pride or stubborn folly. Yet the prevailing tone generally as well as specifically with those who used him as their confessor was one of gentleness and hope. 'No one was more tender and gentle with his penitents (and he heard many confessions), no one more sensitive to the sorrows of others. Yet he was a man of unconquerable hopefulness.'[28] Above all, he was a great encourager, and would often urge a man or woman, 'You must not let temptation take the heart out of you. You must go bravely and quietly on.'[29]

> His sympathy with the tempted and his love
> of souls made him an almost too lenient judge.
> Thankfulness for what had been avoided,
> rather than horror at what had been done,
> was the note of all that he said. In matters of
> Direction too, his tendency was the reverse of
> ascetic. 'In the world, but not of it': 'Using, as
> not abusing.'[30]

After pronouncing formal absolution he would always offer up extempory prayer with wonderful insight and directly and personally applied to the needs and difficulties of the particular penitent.

King did not think it wise to be always preaching about Confession (as was rather a tendency then in some churches), but he liked to preach a definite sermon about it every Lent and every Advent. The conclusion of one such sermon was:

> But, dear people, you will be saying—'this is Roman Catholic'. No, it isn't; there is a difference, and I will tell you what it is. The Roman Catholic Church says you must go to Confession once a year. The English Church says you may go whenever you like.[31]

Similarly, writing to a priest who had sought his advice on this same matter of the confessional, he takes the opportunity to spell out his own position more fully:

> Confession to a priest is not necessary, God will pardon on true repentance; therefore confession of our sins to God, with true sorrow and purpose of amendment, and prayer for pardon through Christ, will bring pardon. The necessity of confession to a priest was not enforced till the Council of Lateran (1215 A.D.) . . . Our Prayer Book says, as you know, in the exhortation to Holy Communion, that if a person cannot find peace in this way, then their duty is to go to the priest for confession. We should, I think, teach the people this, and trust to the Holy Spirit to guide them when to come. In the case of sickness, as you know, we are to move the sick person to make a special confession if there is any weighty matter. Here again, if we all did

this, I think a great number would be able to
see what they ought to do, without any great
difficulty.[32]

In this, as in so many other ways, King's teaching
and practice, both in spiritual counselling as well
as in his specific teaching on the vexed matter of
Confession, is radically different from that of the
Church of Rome: it is all very modest and Anglican,
as well as being utterly faithful to the Prayer Book.
That was typical of King's whole attitude to other
matters such as the liturgy, worship and ritual, as
well as to Confession, and always so deeply pastoral
and thoroughly loyal to the Church of England.

It would seem from everything available—though
of necessity so much of any ministry within the con-
fines of the confessional is by definition 'under the
seal'—that King's pervading optimism concerning
human nature in general held good for those who
sought his ministry in the confessional. Here, as elsewhere in other aspects of his ministry, he exhibits
that 'sane pastoral optimism which so distinctively
characterizes the fourteenth-century English School'
somewhat in contrast with the 'medieval scholastic
and modern Roman systems which regard the confessional primarily as restorative and juridical', while

Anglicanism sees confession primarily as an act
of worship, an expression of penitential love.
The first deals in carefully graded juridical
distinctions, issuing from the mortal-venial
classification, the second makes a generous
prostration at the foot of the Cross; if there is any

question of reinstatement to a lost position, it is
more analogous to the reconciliation of husband
and wife—who have remained 'married' during
estrangement—rather than the acquittal of a
prisoner.[33]

King's, attitude to education and formation sprang
from a very different and more optimistic and affirmative view of human nature: he consistently sought to
draw out from his students, or from those who sought
his spiritual guidance, what was already latent in
them, rather than imposing or inserting pre-packaged
information. 'We truly educate', said King when he
preached at the opening of Keble College Hall and
Library on 25 April 1878, 'when we educe, draw out,
unfold, perfect that common humanity which is in
every man, wherever and whatever he may be.'[34]

In precisely this way, King's influence as a teacher
and pastor was in stark contrast to that of Liddon,
who also, yet in a markedly different way, greatly
influenced his students and those who came to him
for spiritual guidance. As Owen Chadwick writes,
'Liddon perceived with trembling clarity, the deform-
ities of human nature when seen in God's light. King
perceived with a trembling sense of mystery, the
image of God in human nature', albeit 'smudged',
as Gerard Manley Hopkins would have said, yet
never totally overwritten or overridden, but simply
awaiting the discriminating and sensitive 'retouch-
ing' of an experienced artist: such was King's genius
and artistry.

For example, there is no evidence whatever that

King ever used the discipline as it was termed: it would have been totally out of character—'forced' and unnatural from King's more optimistic even humanistic perspective. In this more pastoral rather than juridical understanding of the sacrament of Penance, the emphasis is not so much on the sins, but rather upon affording the penitent the opportunity to reassert and to reaffirm his or her desire to live the virtues of the Christian faith and the evangelical counsels. This is a very important distinction and one that should not be lost.

St Paul knew what it was to struggle with life as a Christian should live it with its implied behavioral contradictions—even hypocrisy, as many would see it—with regard to the way he actually lived it: 'For I do not do the good I want, but the evil I do not want, is what I do' (Romans 7:19).

The opportunity to hold together this apparent contradiction by confessing our sins to God, in the presence of a priest, or a 'third party' as Wesley himself strongly advised and, as indeed, the New Testament encourages, is intended to enable the penitent to hold together both the ideal and goal of all our striving, while at the same time verbalising openly the reality of the contradictory day-to-day sins and failings.

Here is the real tension at the heart of Christian discipleship which pastoral theology at the hands of King, and his distinguished successors and occupants of that same professorial chair in Oxford sought to resolve: a tension between the ultimate moral and ethical ideal as in the evangelical counsels of the New Testament and the apparent reality of recurring sin which in practice 'clings so closely' (Hebrews 12:1) at every stage of the way. We know in our heart of hearts the destination of the journey and that purity of heart by which alone we shall see God, but equally we know that we still have a long way to travel with the hazards of temptation unresisted that can all too easily throw us off course. The challenge throughout the long journey of discipleship is to hold in faith with a 'double grip' of both realism and idealism, 'going on steadily and quietly', as King so often used to say both for himself and to those who sought his guidance, for here, as in so many other respects, it is not a matter of either/or, but rather of both/and, however seemingly contradictory, or even 'hypocritical' that may appear to the uninitiated.

> We can cling to some idealistic image of the way human life should be and spin around unsettled all our life. Or we can give up our ideals and settle in the 'real' and live a rather disappointing or maybe even a profoundly disappointed life. Or we can choose to live in the dynamic and exciting tension of a life that clings to an ideal, still lovingly embracing the 'real' — in oneself and in others and in all else — and gently moving toward the ideal.[35]

Such a mature use of the sacrament of Penance can help enormously in holding this tension, aided by the Grace of the sacrament and enabling the penitent to press forward and not to be overwhelmed by failure.

'Sorrow for sin', says St Bernard, 'is indeed necessary, but it should not involve endless self-preoccupa-
tion. You should dwell also on the glad remembrance
of the loving kindness of God', as St Paul came to
realize, namely that God's grace was sufficient, or,
as in the words of Charles Wesley, the sufficiency
of Grace to cover all my sin: as King affirmed, 'It is
better to be over-charitable than over strict. I am sure
we must run the risk of the charge brought against
our Lord of being too easy with sinners.'[36]

There is a particularly striking example of King's
application of his pastoral theology in a particular
case in his refusal to go along with the entire High
Church Party on the question of remarriage after
divorce. High Churchmen at that time, almost all
to a man, and certainly the party-spirited Church
Union under Halifax's leadership, held rigidly to
the view—many claiming it to be the unqualified
view of Christ's own teaching—that remarriage after
divorce constituted nothing short of adultery, and
therefore automatically barred the divorcee from
Communion. However, only two years before his
death, we see in King and his outspoken utterances
on this very issue, the pastor who as a former professor of moral and pastoral theology is seeking to hold
together the claims of traditional ethics (the 'ideal' if
you like), while at the same time seeking to minister
with compassion, and understanding in particular
cases. At this point and on this vexed issue, we see
King's mind and heart moving in his characteristically pastoral direction, confessing that he himself

was tending towards the view which would transfer the matter from the scriptural absolute ground to the disciplinary ground.

'I think', he concluded, 'such marriages should be treated by the Church under the heading of Discipline, as extending mercy to those in trouble and perplexity . . . There is much to be said for the stricter view, though, as I have said already, under the heading of Discipline and Mercy, I am willing to accept the less strict view.'[37]

As someone said at the time, who was in fact deeply opposed to King's less strict stand on the matter: 'He would *dread* taking a line, which might, even conceivably, be harder than the line our Lord took.'[38]

There are other striking examples of King going beyond the line of duty or of a purely ethical stand in the cases of his ministry to two or three men on death row in the Lincoln prison near to his home in the Old Palace.

A young fisherman from Grimsby was due to be hanged for murdering his wife. The young man was totally ignorant of the Christian faith, but King spent a fortnight before the execution teaching him about the return of the prodigal son. In the end the young man was led to making his confession and to receiving communion at the hands of the bishop, as King remained with him right to the scaffold.

It's as though he always saw the potential for good in everybody and, as he was recorded as saying: 'We must not give up on any soul.'[39]

King spells out this same pastoral care in his Easter preaching for those the world so often regard as hopeless to amend their ways:

> We have known those of whom the world has lost hope, like the prodigal son, or like the man whose name was legion, with whom men were afraid to have anything to do, men who have been branded by society as abandoned and hardened. We have seen what the grace of God can do even with such, changing death into life and turning the hard rock into a standing water, and the flint stone into a springing well.[40]

In this more optimistic approach to Christian formation, once again King reflects St Francis de Sales, with whom he was frequently compared, and with whose writings, notably, the *Introduction to the Devout Life* he was most certainly familiar, and which he also strongly recommended for reading to his students. Francis 'was extremely sensitive to individual differences of temperament and gift and adapted his direction to accommodate these, never expecting too much of those given only moderate talents and capacity. Yet the balance in his spirituality leans towards optimism and shows a trust in human and divine resources to bring all things into the fullness of their potential.'[41]

THE TRANSFORMING POWER OF PRAYER

King's spirituality in every respect, definitely focused upon the interior life, especially the heart, as being the place of encounter with God. There in the inner realm, for King, was the source of the 'sap' of Grace—amazing Grace—which always makes possible human transformation and where it should have its proper beginning. But he did not espouse the practice of rigid devotional exercises or highly structured interior regimes of any kind, but rather to cultivate a freedom to follow the voice of God that is discerned uniquely in each individual.

It would seem from his approach to what he termed making our bible reading 'more real' and by not 'stopping short' with the written word, but rather allowing it to point and lead beyond to an encounter with the Living Word, that he taught from what was most likely his own practice, that ancient method of praying the scriptures traditionally termed *lectio divina*. From what we can glean from his lecture notes, and here again like de Sales, King would have been generally supportive of a simple wordless type of prayer, and advocating in the words of Francis's great friend Jane de Chantal, that 'the great method of prayer was to have no method at all'—that *higgledy piggledy* (King's words) approach of King, who was always so suspicious of over systematizing development and growth, as he explicitly says of the life of Cuddesdon during his time as principal.

> When the Holy Spirit has taken possession of the person who prays, it does as it pleases without any more need for rules and methods. The soul must be in God's hands like clay in the hands of a potter, so that he might fashion

all parts. Or the soul must be like soft wax to receive a seal's impression.[42]

SPIRITUAL COUNSELLING AND TODAY'S CHURCH

A later distinguished successor to King in the same Chair of Pastoral and Moral Theology, Kenneth Kirk, who like King also went on to be a bishop, in his great classic study of moral theology — *The Vision of God* — the very book that King himself could well have written, claimed:

> The aim of moral theology is . . . to accumulate from every available source whatever informa-tion will be of use to the priest for his task of shepherding individual souls.[43]

And such was the aim of the teaching in the theolog-ical colleges which took their brief from King's Cud-desdon, like the Theological College or Bishop's Hos-tel at Lincoln founded by King's predecessor, Bishop Christopher Wordsworth, the nephew of William Wordsworth, the favoured poet of King. Preaching at the first festival of the newly founded theological college in Lincoln, King, as bishop and Visitor to the College, reflected on the purpose of such a college. He was adamant that such training should involve so very much more than a knowledge of academic theology, and not least for the clergy whose prime duty was the cure of souls and Christian formation:

It is the object of our College to prepare men

for the Divine ministry of Christ's Church, to continue that Divine organization of the Christian ministry which the Preface to our Ordinal asserts to have been in the Church 'from the Apostles' time . . . To be a theologian indeed requires many gifts and special opportunities such as possibly can rarely be found except in our Universities or in our cathedral cities, but this is not necessary for the parish priest; his business is the cure of souls. He will indeed require the knowledge of all theology to a certain degree — dogmatic theology, moral theology, and the scientific adaptation of them both to the needs of individual souls, which we call ascetic theology . . . We need men who, by the power of the Holy Spirit, have comprehended something of the breadth, length, depth, and height of the love of Christ which passeth knowledge; men who are rooted and grounded in and constrained by this love; men who will be patient with sinners and those who are ignorant, and careless, and 'out of the way' . . . men who will love and not grow cold, but who, having loved, like Jesus, will 'love to the end'.[44]

So, what has happened to the teaching of pastoral theology in today's Church? We may well ask. Where and how would such a concept be used, let alone taught? In the last century, Thomas C. Oden commented specifically on the absence in modern pastoral counselling literature of any interest in the classical models of pastoral care and the cure of souls:

Recent pastoral counselling has incurred a fixated dependency and indebtedness to modern psychology and to modern consciousness generally that has prevented it from even

> looking at pre-modern wisdoms of most kinds
> including classical pastoral care... We have bet
> all our chips on the assumption that modern
> consciousness will lead us into vaster freedom,
> while our specific freedom to be attentive to the
> Christian pastoral tradition has been plundered,
> polemicized and despoiled.[45]

Surely, it is all too clear that the clergy cannot help others along the royal highway of that inner journey of the Spirit unless they themselves have not only been taught it, but are also themselves seeking to live by it and by travelling along on the same journey of discipleship and transformation, from 'one degree of glory to another'.

It is in this aspect of the training and the equipping of the clergy for this particular ministry of Christian formation and reconciliation, that we need to revisit King and, in the words of Rowan Williams, to share King's lifelong concern 'to train a clergy' to be 'pastorally, theologically and humanly competent at a different level of professionalism from what [has] been so widely taken for granted before'[46] — *mutatis mutandis* and even more demonstrably in our own day, we might wish to add, 'for too long'.

8

The Universal Call to Holiness of Life

The true work of the Church is to bring men and women to that perfection it is intended they should reach in holiness and holy living.[1]

THE NATURE OF HOLINESS

In Lincoln Cathedral, on 24 May 1935, a special service was held to mark the fiftieth anniversary of King's consecration as a bishop in the Church of God. Archbishop Cosmo Gordon Lang, the last of the patrician and princely archbishops, celebrated a solemn Eucharist and addressed the huge congregation on 'Edward King, Bishop and Saint'. The Collect, Epistle and Gospel were specifically prepared for the occasion of what is still observed as the 'Commemoration of Edward King', and have been used in the Lincoln diocese and widely throughout the Church annually on 8 March to mark the anniversary of his death.

In that sermon, Lang spoke of his own personal encounters with King and the impact it had made on him at a specific turning point in his life when, as a young man, he was struggling to discern his vocation—should it be the bar or ordination to the priesthood? The occasion of that decisive meeting was further reinforced early the following morning, when he was confirmed by King in his private chapel at Lincoln. In a letter to his mother describing his Confirmation, the youthful Lang speaks of King as 'one of the most saintly and delightful of men', and as having 'the Divine light in his eyes'.[2]

Many years later, that same claim was further reiterated and articulated, but this time, not from the pen of that same young Fellow of All Souls' College, Oxford, but now with the authority and from the lips of the Primate of all England, in memorable words from the pulpit of what had formerly been King's own cathedral: King, Lang unequivocally proclaimed, was 'the most saintly of men, and the most human of saints'.

RECOGNIZING HOLINESS

Cosmo Gordon Lang could not have been from a more radically different 'stable' —socially, politically or theologically—from that of the saintly King, and yet he saw in King, as indeed did so many of King's contemporaries, the undeniable marks of holiness. The struggle begins however when, any attempts are made to categorize such 'marks' or signs, to vindicate and authenticate any claims to sanctity, as Lang so demonstrably did for Edward King.

In an age like our own, there will always be a plentiful supply of those who would all too willingly come forward as the devil's advocates, to disqualify any potential 'candidates' who are up for canonization or beatification, by all too readily pointing out the flaws and failings. Yet, no one, however saintly, is totally free from the blind spots of their contemporary cultural conditioning, the limitations of the age in which they have lived, or the genes they have inherited, and, in that way, King is no exception.

For, in honouring the saints, we are most definitely not claiming them to be specimens of flawless humanity or morally sanitized beyond reproach. 'A human being is holy not because he or she triumphs by will-power over chaos and guilt and leads a flawless life', writes Rowan Williams, 'but because that life shows the victory of God's faithfulness in the midst of disorder and imperfection.'[3]

When people encounter a saintly person and seek to communicate to others the nature of that occasion or encounter, the vocabulary they use is invariably strained as when similarly attempting to convey impressions after the performance of a great piece of music, or the viewing of a great work of art: holiness, like beauty and love, is primarily experienced, stubbornly defying analysis.

Scott Holland, one of King's many close friends, attempting to communicate his experience of times spent with King, characteristically seems to go into verbal overdrive:

Twice I went down to the Lincoln Fair with him, all among the cocoa-nuts, and the ginger-bread, and the fat women. It was a delicious experience, to note the affection that followed him about. He drew out love, as the sun draws fragrance from the flowers. He moved in an atmosphere of love.[4]

It took a Lincolnshire shepherd who worked with his sheep on the Lincolnshire Wolds, to spot this 'beyondness' in King (for the want of a better word), which more analytical minds could well miss. On meeting and talking with King, during one of the bishop's many visits to the far-flung villages and parishes of his huge diocese, the shepherd is reputed to have said, doubtless with a broad Lincolnshire accent, 'Eh! then yours is a yon-side religion, I see, sir'.[5]

Perhaps for brevity and simplicity's sake, Michael Ramsey gets nearer the mark when, rather after the manner of King himself, he said with his characteristic gift for saying profound things simply: 'The saints make God real.'

THE FACE OF HOLINESS

In seeking to trace the source and nature of holiness, some words of Pope John Paul II offer a helpful insight: 'Holiness, a message that convinces without the need for words, is the living reflection of the face of Christ',[6] and it was with the light and beauty of

King's face, especially in his later years, that so many of his friends and contemporaries were so forcefully struck and found to be so compellingly attractive.

Scott Holland, admittedly and characteristically in that same verbal overdrive, vividly recalls:

> Those eyes of his were an illumination . . . Was there ever such a face, so gracious, so winning, so benignant, so tender? Its beauty was utterly natural and native. It made no effort to be striking, or marked, or peculiar, or special. It possessed just the typical beauty that should, of right, belong to the human countenance. It seemed to say, 'This is what a face is meant to be. This is the face that a man would have if he were, really, himself. This is the face that love would normally wear.[7]

And again: 'The voice was almost ladylike in its gentleness, and the whole face was, from time to time, suffused by a smile which lit it up, as a ray of sunshine lights a quiet landscape. That smile was the outward token of the inner life of God.'[8]

Like a sacrament or an icon, the outward and visible facial features—'that smile', which Scott Holland describes—derive their character from what is hidden, namely 'the inner life of God', and from 'a life-long communion with God', as in the words of the chaplain to the Guild of St Barnabas, of which King was the patron:

> It is no extravagance to say that it did them [the nurses] good even to look at him. One of the kindliest of men by native temperament, his *life-long communion with God had touched*

his genial face with a light, a sweetness, and a
spiritual beauty that charmed all who saw him,
poor as well as rich, old and young.[9]

A 'lifelong communion with God', that surely was
and is the secret of the saints—the outward and visible testifying to the inward character—(or 'inscape'
to use that evocative word of Gerard Manley Hopkins)—of our hidden self, so that, as Christ both
encouraged as well as cautioned, 'there is nothing
hidden that shall not be revealed' (Matthew 10:26).
'Your face is the icon of your life', says John O'Donohue. 'In the human face a life looks out at the world
and also looks in on itself.'[10]

THE BEAUTY OF HOLINESS

It is in that inward look in depth in times of prayer
alone with God, and the workings of the Spirit which
probes the inner nature of ourselves, that the real
work of transformation is done. Any outward beauty
is all of a piece with the other two marks of the divine
character, namely goodness and truth. True prayer
rising from the inner life of the Spirit, reveals the hidden things of God, and so there is no quick cosmetic
fix if the outward and visible is truly to show forth
the inner transforming work of Grace. Those 'inner
probings' defy any hint of escapism and are hugely
demanding and even ruthless in that search for truth
and true godliness, as in the words of Yeats: 'Man
needs reckless courage to descend into the abyss

of himself.'[11] In one of the Collects in the Book of Common Prayer we are taught to pray that God will 'Graft in our hearts the love of Thy name; increase in us true religion':[12] all true religion proceeds from within the heart.

So, when the psalmist speaks of 'the beauty of holiness' (Psalm 96:9), it is of that outward beauty which is derived from the inner life of goodness and truth—in a word from those 'of a pure heart'. It was of such a form of beauty that so many who encountered King, consistently spoke—a beauty, which has nothing to do with cosmetics, a beauty the world cannot replicate.

> Modern culture is obsessed with cosmetic perfection. Beauty is standardized; it has become another product for sale. In its real sense, beauty is the illumination of your soul.[13]

BALANCE—NATURALNESS

Yet, however much King's contemporaries empha-size his holiness of life and his otherworldliness, they always affirm the balance and naturalness and the humanity of his sanctity, as in the words of Lang's sermon; the unaffectedness of King's disposition in every facet of his character:

> So typical was its naturalness. Yet, of course, this did not diminish its intense individuality. It was only that this most vital individuality was so whole and sound and normal and true,

that it seemed to be the perfect expression of what a man might be. Throughout, one was conscious of this rounded normality. There was nothing in him one-sided, or excessive or unbalanced. There was no side of his character which wanted explanation, or was out of perspective. Everything hung together. Everything befitted. He never overshot his mark: or fell below it ... No note was forced. No pose was taken ... Grace had so intermingled with nature that it was all of one piece.[14]

It's the contemplatives, like King, with their non-dualistic worldview who best demonstrate this balance in their lives, holding together in the dynamic unity of the Holy Spirit what so often the world perceives as irreconcilable opposites. In order to keep that balance, there is a need to hold, admittedly at times, in tension, the interior and the exterior, the imminent and visible together with the invisible and the transcendent, in a 'wisdom' in the words of Christ, which can 'bring out of its treasure both things old and new' (Matthew 13:52). There's a sense in which this is wholesome, healthy and something of what we mean by holy.

Such a 'balance' for King, as for his great mentor, Bishop Sailer of Regensburg, and which was of special importance to both alike, was a balance specifically between heart and mind. Indeed for King, the domination of the intellect at the expense of other human faculties such as intuition and notably experience, constituted the greatest barrier to faith and to enjoying true communion with God in the Spirit of prayer and self-transcendence.

> High spiritual truth is not gained by the intellect by itself, for when it has done its utmost, the affections of the heart have to be aroused, so that all our faculties may be lifted up by the power of the Holy Spirit into communion with God, for we have the capability, even in this world, of enjoying real communion with God.[15]

Similarly for King, ascesis or discipline did not imply anything negative or gloomy, as it tended to do for Newman, Pusey and Liddon or even Gladstone. Within King was a spring of joy—that fruit of the Spirit second only to love—welling up continually, as fresh as it was inexhaustible. In his speaking and writings, joy was never far away, and his letters sparkle, frequently punctuated with humour and that lightness of touch, which characterized all his dealings.

'Brightness' was one of King's favourite words with regard to the Christian life together with 'glowing' as one of his characteristic adjectives. Bishop Walsham How, who had observed King giving meditations spoke of King's 'loving, beautiful brightness of manner'.[16] Pope Benedict XIV laid down the requirements needed for canonization as being three traditional marks of sainthood: popular cultus, three miracles, three heroic acts, to which perhaps joy, which after all, is second only to love as listed in the 'fruits of spirit', should be added.

Baron von Hügel claimed incisively that it is precisely 'spiritual joy' which distinguishes the saint from the saintly—the canonized from the beatified, if you like—going on to comment how he 'used to wonder', in his frequent conversations with Newman, 'how one so good and who had made so many sacrifices to God, could be so depressing' and even going on to assert that 'Newman could indeed be beatified—saintly though undoubtedly he was—though not canonized as a "saint"'.[17]

DIVISIONS OF CHURCHMANSHIP

There is a further holding together of what so many perceive as opposites, which becomes apparent in any study of Edward King, as with many others of saintly life. In the Church of King's day the Evangelicals of the Church Association and the Anglo-Catholics of the Church Union were in hostile opposition resulting, in King's case, in the meaningless Lincoln Judgement of 1890. The paradox is of course, that so many of those who in later life, belonged to the High Church party, began life as Evangelicals. Bishop Samuel Wilberforce, who had been brought up under the influence of his father William Wilberforce who was a stern evangelical, is but one of many such prominent persons in the Catholic revival in the Church of England. Although Wilberforce admired and indeed practised much of what the Tractarians taught and believed, influenced as he undoubtedly was by his time at Oriel, along with his brothers and his brother-in-law, Manning, yet 'he never lost his reverence for the evangelicals who had taught him a personal trust in a loving Saviour',[18] issuing in works and action for the common good, all of which had been so characteristic of his distinguished father.

MENTORS AT ORIEL—WESLEY— BROTHERHOOD—HOLY CLUB

It is clear from any reading of King's early life that his quest for holiness of life had made an indelible mark, even from his earliest years. During his time as an undergraduate at Oriel College, as well as falling under the influence of such holy men as Charles Marriott, in whom the young King undoubtedly saw a genuine Tractarian sanctity and a 'discipline unto holiness' along with the saintly and scholarly Richard Church, King became a member of the Brotherhood of the Holy Trinity. The Brotherhood enjoined a simple rule of life upon its members, originally drawn up by Pusey, and all in the pursuit of holiness of life, with aims not dissimilar from those of the Holy Club formed by Wesley during the previous century, which encouraged a similar holiness of life, or to use Wesley's words 'an inner holiness' and an 'inward Christianity as opposed to outward and 'conventional Christianity'.

The Rule of the Brotherhood of the Holy Trinity represented the core spirituality of Catholic Anglicanism, that same spirituality which King had observed in the lives of his Oriel mentors—Marriott and Richard Church—setting theological study within the wider context of a disciplined inner life, nurtured by personal prayer, scripture and the sacraments and issuing in simplicity of life, service in the community (with particular reference to caring for the needs of the poor), and the 'tithing' of income 'for God's service'.

The Rule explicitly impressed the need to 'rise an hour before the time of morning chapel, with a view to devoting the interval to private prayers'. As for sacramental Confession, that perennial bone of contention for critics of the Catholic revival in Anglicanism, the Rule as devised by Pusey was totally in accordance with the teaching of the Book of Common Prayer and the Anglican tradition generally, by advising its use, and the opening of one's 'grief to a priest', only 'if the conscience be troubled'.

WESLEY AND THE CALL FOR PERFECTION

We have traced throughout this study of King's spirituality the close affinity that he felt for Wesley and the whole Methodist 'awakening', an affinity which even predated his arrival in Lincoln as bishop in 1885, when he had spoken so enthusiastically about becoming bishop in 'John Wesley's diocese', as he referred to it. The Lincoln diocesan magazine, which King himself had founded, reported the following year: 'On November 30th, 1886 Dr King gave a lecture on John Wesley at Sheffield for the Church Lecture Society.' After giving a sketch of the great Lincolnshire worthy, he commended the respect which the Wesleyans pay to the religious enthusiasm of the young. He also commended Wesley for his emphasis on the doctrine of 'perfection'.[19] Clearly, King saw in Wesley's teaching on, what Wesley usually referred to as 'perfection' as his own lifelong pursuit of that which is more usually termed 'sanctification' or 'holiness'. Even back as far as his years as professor in Oxford we find in the notes of those lectures, frequent references to Wesley and his call for 'perfection'.

'I fancy it was the doctrine of "perfection" that was part of John Wesley's power, "Here is a man who calls us to be perfect"',[20] King is on record as saying in one of his lectures, presumably totally unselfconsciously and unaware of how such an acclaim could equally be said of himself.

For King, along with Wesley, saw religion as nothing less than a 'constant ruling habit of soul; a renewal of our minds in the image of God, a recovery of the divine likeness'.[21] The Holy Club formed in 1729, while John Wesley was still a Fellow of Lincoln College, and encouraged his followers to live under some kind of General Rule (initially drawn up by Wesley). In several respects, such as 'early rising for personal prayer and frequent Communion', it bears similarities to the Rule of the Brotherhood: in short, 'the underlying ideals of the Oxford Methodists at least in Wesley's eyes were intended to reflect a total imitation of Christ'—or, to use a consistent and recurring phrase of King's, to become more 'Christ-like Christians'.

In a sermon entitled, *The Circumcision of the Heart*, which Wesley preached in 1733, he set out his ideal of 'Christian perfection', the goal and end to which all the disciplines of a Christian life-style and disci-pleship should point and lead. Wesley defines 'cir-cumcision of the heart' as 'that habitual disposition of soul, which in the sacred writings is termed holiness ... the being cleansed from sin' and 'so renewed in the image of our mind' as to be 'perfect as our Father in heaven is perfect'.[22]

Both in the Oxford of the Wesleys in the eighteenth century and the Oxford of King the following century, where 'Conventional Christianity' as Wesley termed it, still held sway as also in the country at large, such a disciplined life and commitment would have been held in ridicule: 'enthusiasm' in matters religious was somewhat taboo. Predictably, the Holy Club acquired a variety of nicknames, mostly derisory, especially from Christ Church and Merton men: names such as 'Enthusiasts', 'Sacramentarians' (because of Wesley's practice of frequent Communion), 'The Reforming Club' and the 'Godly Club'.

Little wonder that King was not ashamed to be associated and indeed supportive of the many Meth-odists in his diocese. The content of his teaching, which was always gospel-centred, and which drew richly on scripture, led many from differing tradi-tions, and not least the numerous Methodists, to speak warmly of him.

> Descendants of the men whom John Wesley
> had converted recognized that in their new
> bishop they had a man of God, who lived in
> prayer and preached Christ Crucified. This was
> what they wanted, and his sermons were often
> punctuated by ejaculations of 'Ah!' 'Hallelujah!'
> and 'Praise the Lord!' in the true fashion of the
> Methodists.[23]

It seems that people of varying traditions in the diocese soon came to value and appreciate King's simple, direct, evangelical style of preaching, as one person was reported as saying, in a strong Lincolnshire accent, after hearing him preach—'He's nowt but an owd Methody'.[24]

It was precisely Wesley's criticism of the prevailing 'Conventional Christianity' which would have rung so many bells with King, who, like Wesley, saw both the scriptures and the Person of Christ as the true benchmark of what makes for a truly, Christ-like Christian, rather than one measured by the standards of the world.

> What does the Bible say is the true standard
> of holiness for individual Christians? Brethren
> are we not in danger of contenting ourselves
> by the false standard of mutual comparison,
> measuring ourselves by ourselves . . . we are
> content to walk in the light of sparks of our own
> kindling; we are content to take our standard
> of holiness from the prevailing customs and
> opinions of the present Christian world instead
> of going to the law and to the testimony, instead
> of looking at the Book which God himself has
> given us for our guidance. The question for the

believing Christian ought surely to be, not what man says, but what does God say?[25]

And again, in another of his Easter sermons:

> Let us not be content to take our standard of life from the present condition even of the Christian part of the world, but let us go back to the Scriptures and search them, and ask the risen Saviour to help us to understand them aright.[26]

And even more powerfully in words that could equally have been spoken from the mouth of Wesley, the previous century:

> We have regained, I thankfully believe, a real position in morals . . . But real and great as this moral progress has been, it is just here that with all humility, but with the most sincere earnestness, I am anxious to ask you to consider the application of my text . . . The new forces in society, the newly extended political power among those who constitute the middle and lower classes of modern society, and the increased power of *pleasure* in *all* classes, are so strong that there is a danger that . . . modern society may still preserve the form and phraseology of Christianity, but lose, if not deny, the power of it.[27]

SALESIAN SPIRITUALITY—FRIENDSHIP WITH
GOD—CHRIST-CENTRED

The person of Christ and King's Christo-centric spirituality, so evident throughout this whole study, might not only be said as above of Wesley with his insistence on holiness and what he termed 'perfection', but equally and also, of St Francis de Sales, with whom even in his own day, King was often so favourably compared.

Certainly, Salesian spirituality, as in the writings and letters of St Francis de Sales and in particular in Francis's spiritual classic—*Introduction to the Divine Life*—were all alike well known to King, as well as being commended by King to his students.

Both for King and for Francis, the Person of Jesus is central to their whole inner life of the Spirit. At the head of the letters that Jane de Chantal, the great friend of Francis, wrote, as well as in the words that Francis himself penned, are repeatedly the words: 'Live Jesus!'

> To 'Live Jesus' is to have – in Francis de Sales's words—the name of Jesus engraved on one's heart. It was to allow that name to become one's own true name, to allow one's entire self—body, thoughts, affections, actions, decisions, work, devotion—to be animated by the reality of the person known by that name. To allow Jesus to live, one did not simply learn about Jesus or pray to Jesus or even imitate Jesus. One surrendered the vital centre of one's being—one's heart, as understood in the holistic biblical sense—to another living presence. [28]

This Christocentric spirituality of course is by no means restricted to the spirituality of the likes of King and de Sales, although it is especially explicit in both their teaching, and the spiritual formation they nurtured as well as aspired to themselves. In the case of Francis, his ministry as a Catholic bishop was 'in the regions of the unbelievers', where he was appointed to care for the diocese of Annecy in which the city of Calvin's Geneva lay. It was in that challenging setting that Francis consistently pleaded the love and all-sufficient Grace of Christ, while in the case of King, his message sought to lift the ethical deism of the previous century to the theism of a personal relationship with the God, revealed in the face of Christ.

King was always insistent that the person of Christ is more to the Christian disciple than merely an example of a godly life, as so typically expressed, in the Rugby of Arnold in what is sometimes termed 'public-school religion', with its insistence on the morality of duty and obedience—two of the seven words in King's outline of the spiritual journey. But for King, such a religion lacked the other five means of Grace, as outlined earlier, and in particular the sacraments of the Church;[29] a right reading of scripture and personal prayer, centred in the person of Christ. From King's perspective there was the need to go much further so that not just the example of Christ is taken on board, but also the plenitude of the gospel truth that all are called to be made partakers in the life of Christ himself, in whom, and as children of the same heavenly Father, we directly partake in the very life of God.

King is repeatedly explicit about this, as here in one of his Easter Sermons:

This two-fold relation to the risen and ascended
Saviour is essential to the right understanding
of the Christian religion. Christ is our example,
and Christ is our life. This truth is essential as
in the Collect when we pray that we may 'both
follow the example of Christ's patience, and
also be made partakers of His Resurrection'.
To follow the example of His patience: that
is to make Christ our example; so as to be
partakers of His Resurrection: that is to make
Christ our life.

We find the same Christ-centred spirituality in the
exhortation of de Sales, when he speaks in a similar
manner of the need, not only to follow the example
of Christ, but also in his words, to take on the 'reality
of the life' that Christ lived and is:

> Undergirding all Christian spiritual traditions
> is the insistence that human beings, to be true
> to their deepest insights, must follow the way
> to God opened for them by Jesus of Nazareth,
> in some way taking on the reality of the life
> he lived . . . The entire progress of the human
> endeavour is thus articulated with a language
> (both verbal and pictorial) fashioned from
> the paradigmatic life, death and resurrection
> of Jesus Christ. The question, 'How does
> Jesus live?' could therefore be asked of any
> Christian spirituality. The answers would differ
> depending on the ways in which individuals
> or groups of believers understand *who* Jesus is
> and the way in which they envision the process
> of ridding the self of obstacles that are in the
> way of Jesus's showing forth.[30]

Of course, all this is thoroughly Pauline, with his

dictum, 'I no longer live, but Christ lives in me', but it is also at the core of the distinctive Salesian inscription as a presence to be 'experienced', a reality to be 'lived' as it is likewise no less prominent in the language of both Wesley and King, with their emphasis on 'experience' as a further extension of reason: for de Sales and his friend, Jane de Chantal, 'authentic human existence was identified by them as the continual and ever-present bringing to life of the living Lord who bears the name Jesus'.[31]

Such, it would seem was the nature of that intimate relationship of friendship and companionship with the person of Christ, which King both taught and exemplified, and to which, as we have seen, in an earlier chapter, the English school of spirituality characteristically professes.

A further element latent in Francis's vision and his spirituality and again somewhat in line with that of both Wesley and King, is the idea of 'perfection' or the process of sanctification as King would have normally referred to it—or even better still, as in King's own, often repeated short-hand—becoming 'more Christ-like Christians'. Wesley lightly revised his understanding of perfection over the years when later he seems to emphasize perfection as being an ongoing process, rather than a one-off moment of conversion, leaving room for the possibility of further occasions for further 'awakening' experiences. Bishop Francis, and again so very like King,

> most certainly believed in the possibility of human perfection, but his insistence on

indifference as a seminal principle in the spiritual life tended to downplay any zealous quest for perfection or inordinate concern for the achievement of a 'perfect' spiritual state.[32]

HOLINESS AND PERFECTION—THEOSIS

'It is God alone who is the perfect man' (or 'man as he ought to be'), asserts the Greek Orthodox writer, Philip Sherrard. 'Only God is completely and utterly human. In so far as man fails to realize the divine in himself, to that extent he falls short of being completely human. He remains less than human. His human nature is truncated, just as the divine nature is truncated and less than divine if it is not humanized in Christ.'[33]

King was consistently clear 'that human nature has not got perfection in itself, apart from God',[34] and yet, in his preaching of the Easter Gospel he was equally insistent:

> We ought today to set before ourselves the standard of moral and spiritual perfection, and to consider the words of the Saviour in the Sermon on the Mount as having a practical bearing on our daily conduct: 'Be ye perfect, even as your Father in heaven is perfect.'[35]

In that same Easter Sermon—*Spiritual Lives*—King continues to insist that it is precisely the victory of Easter, which should 'renew our hope in ourselves, in our striving after holiness', rather than 'giving away to despair and accepting the lower level of the present condition as the limit of the excellence which we can reach . . . It is for us today, when we stand before the empty grave and empty tomb, to think of that triumphant perfection which has been attained for man by Christ taking of the manhood into God.' [36]

Once again we see King spelling out the danger—in his frequently repeated aphorism—of 'stopping short' and settling for the assurance of justification rather than pressing on to claim our full inheritance as children of God in that ongoing process of sanctification and perfection whereby we may become partakers of the divine life:

'The Spirit beareth witness with our spirit; when God gives the love of Himself, to will to be His, the Spirit whereby we call Him Father, we cannot but doubt but that he accepts, pardons, justifies, and will finally glorify and perfect the believer', finally hammering home with gospel confidence that 'Christ will finish his work IN us, which He has finished FOR us, so as to present us whole without spot to the Father'.[37]

It was King's life and presence even more than his teaching and pastoral ministry, whether as spiritual guide or confessor which vindicated such spiritually triumphant claims with the most compelling evidence of such claims that 'the divine has been humanized' once and for all in the person of Christ, who came to show us God's way of being fully human. King consistently contended that the invitation to be 'partakers of the Divine life', is open for our humanity, in the here-and-now, and not only in the hereafter, to be experienced and at least partially realized, in what the Orthodox Churches of the East refer to as *theosis* or *divinization*. Although the vocabulary with King is different, the intention is clearly identical:

> The language of Scripture justifies our highest aspirations. It tells us that we may be partakers of the Divine nature, that we may become members of Christ, that Christ can dwell in us, that the Spirit of Christ can be in us. Nay, the Saviour has said: 'If a man love me, my Father will love him, and We will come and make our abode with him.'[38]

Indeed, there are some who would ask 'whether the primary clue to understanding the basic intuitions' of the founding fathers of the Oxford Movement, is to be found 'in seeing it as a sudden epiphany within the Christian West, of the prayer, the vision, and the theology of the Greek Fathers. In a remarkable way, since their direct contacts with Eastern Orthodoxy were minimal, they succeeded in penetrating into its ethos. The doctrine of *theosis* is the key to understanding their whole vision of Christian faith and life. Without understanding that, we shall grasp little of the inspiration behind'[39] the Oxford Movement, or indeed, one might add, behind the inner life of King, which was to have such a far-ranging influence on the wider Church in succeeding generations.

It is significant that Cranmer gave faint hints to that same process of divine in-dwelling in the more restrained words of the Prayer of Humble Access in the Book of Common Prayer, when communicants pray that 'we may evermore dwell in Him, and He in us'.

ECUMENISM AND HOLINESS

For King, the whole question of the restoration of the visible unity of the wider Church was inextricably bound up with the question of holiness and of that perfection in God whereby the prayer of Christ could be fulfilled: 'That they may be one, even as we are one; I in them, and Thou in Me, that they may be perfected into one.'

King claimed that in that text from 'the great passage in that Holy of Holies of Holy Scripture, the 17th chapter of St John':

> We have the great assurance that the desire of our hearts is *real*. Unity is the true goal to which we are pressing, and it shall *be; koinonia* is the natural end of *philia*, but it has been well pointed out here that if we take our Lord's words as a pledge of what one day shall be, we must be careful to follow our Lord's example. He speaks of unity, but He speaks of it in prayer. He prays for it: 'Neither for these only do I pray, but for them also that believe on Me through their word; that they all may be one.[40]

King was manifestly clear, that for the Church to be

'one' it must also be 'holy', sharing in and partaking in nothing less than the risen life of Christ. Put another way, only the Church which, in the words of the creeds, is 'holy' can ever be 'one' Church: the concluding words of the creeds as being 'one, holy, catholic and apostolic Church' constitute a package deal. Visible and organic unity could not be achieved by reshuffling doctrines and dogmas by way of accommodating differing views, but rather by a renewal in holiness of life rooted and grounded in nothing less than, or short of that unity of the Spirit proceeding from the Father and the Son, in whom all will be one.

Furthermore, as in King's enthronement sermon, at the outset of his time in Lincoln, 'reconciliation', in a word, was the mission to which he had called his diocese—reconciliation in the fullest possible sense of the word: 'what he wanted to do in the diocese was to draw men to Christ, that they might be nearer to God, and nearer to each other in the unity of His Holy Church'.[41]

King had clearly perceived, as in a letter written in 1906, that the Church of England had only itself to blame for the separation and growth of Methodists precisely because of what was so clearly lacking in the Established Church of his day, by way of spiritual depth and holiness of life:

> I need hardly say I have never had any harsh feeling towards Nonconformists, and, I might add, especially not towards Wesleyans and Primitive Methodists, because I have always

felt that it was the want of spiritual life in the
Church and brotherly love which led them to
separate. The more we can draw near to Christ
ourselves and fill ourselves with His Spirit, the
greater power we shall have for unity. What
we want is more *Christlike Christians*. May God
guide and bless your efforts to draw all nearer
to Him, and in Him to one another.[42]

Archbishop Michael Ramsey, in a typically profound
sermon preached at the Faith and Order Conference in Nottingham in 1964, spoke of how at the
deepest levels in the life of faith and discipleship, in
expressions of devotion and in a deeper contemplative spirituality, it is often the case that ecclesiastical
traditions so often perceived superficially as being
widely opposed and separated, nevertheless find
themselves surprisingly close together:

In a depth below doctrinal thought and
structure, heart speaks to heart. May there not
be, to give another instance, a similar apartness
in the realm of thought and nearness in depth
of religious meaning in the case of some of
the cleavages about faith, justification and the
sacraments.[43]

It is precisely and solely because King perceived
the recovery of the visible unity of the Church as
the Body of Christ, as being an organic communion
of the Spirit, rather than of organizational joinery,
achieved through agreement in matters of dogma
and doctrine, that he was able to point to an appropriate diversity in such a unity, together with an
appropriate diversity through a further development

and unfolding of the life of the mystical Body of Christ. In this, as in other matters, King was ahead of his age and precisely because he had not 'stopped short' — to use his recurring phrase — with the contemporary, westernized outward form of the Church in his day, but pointed forward in faith.

This is most clearly evident in his concluding words to the Lambeth bishops at that Quiet Day, prior to the Lambeth Conference of 1897, in which there is so much of 'vintage' King.

> The idea of the Church as the body should suggest holiness in ourselves . . . It should lead us not to be suspicious of, but to welcome, the diversity of gifts; it should teach us not to require the outward expression of Christianity to be exactly the same, but to allow a liberty for difference of race and class. India and Japan and China may well have their own contributions to offer for the perfecting of the Body of Christ.[44]

MINISTRY AND HOLINESS

Throughout the years when King was directly involved in ministerial formation, both at Cuddesdon and during his years in Oxford, it was this essential link between the truth of the Gospel message and the authenticity of those called to be its messenger, which were constantly asserted in his teaching and preaching. For what was most injurious and dangerous to the Tractarians in general and which could equally be said no less with regard to King himself, 'was inauthentic Christian living. But if [the clergy] could begin to live lives of sanctification—if their lives could evidence the differences in purity and charity that Christianity was supposed to make—then at least the authenticity if not the truth of Christian believing could be seen.'[45]

'The Bible taught the Oxford Movement's leaders that holiness of life is the pathway to the Lord's presence. "Follow peace with all men and holiness, without which no man shall see the Lord" (Hebrews 12: 14). Holiness and its disciplines brought the gift of the vision of God's otherwise invisible kingdom',[46] and vindicated all the claims for the effectiveness of the gospel the clergy proclaimed. In short, 'A Christlike clergy', as King consistently maintained, 'would make it so much easier for the people to believe that we are what we are'.

As Evelyn Underhill wrote, echoing similar sentiments with respect to the clergy:

> The man whose life is coloured by prayer, whose loving communion with God comes first, will always win souls; because he shows them in his own life and person the attractiveness of reality, the demand, the transforming power of the spiritual life.[47]

So it followed that the pastoral preacher must be steeped in prayer and, in King's own words, 'constantly striving for holiness', and it was that further requirement which gave to King's teaching and preaching alike its authority and authenticity.

This message had perhaps taken hold even more firmly in the Lincoln days with King's close relationship with the Lincoln Theological College of which he was the episcopal Visitor and which was only a matter of five minutes' walk or so from the Old Palace. In an address to the students:

> In the day of technical or departmental education, the demand made upon the clergy is, not unreasonably, 'ministerial efficiency'. They should be fitted for their own work in order that they may be 'workmen who need not to be ashamed'. This implies, no doubt, many things, but the centre of it all, without which the rest is practically useless, is 'personal holiness'.

'How are we to do that?' asks King. The reply: 'By reclaiming the reality of the power and resources given to us by the Holy Spirit.'

> We need to keep before ourselves this standard of personal Christian ethics, and to consider the *reality* of the new forces which have been given to us through the Spirit, by which the new standard may be attained—'For we are His workmanship, created in Christ Jesus for good works' (Ephesians 2:10).

And so it follows:

> We need men . . . who have thought out, as far as they can, their own relation to God, and who have realized the strength of the complex proof on which it depends, men who have walked in the threefold light of their own faculties, of revelation, and of the Church, and have seen how the three agree and lead back to *one*.

We need men who have disciplined their reason by endeavouring to discern and speak the exact truth, without fear of the reproof of man, and without the desire of his praise.

We need men who have endeavoured to keep a conscience void of offence, not only in the sight of men, but of God . . .

We need men. . . who are rooted and grounded in and constrained by [Christ's] love; men who will be patient with sinners and those who are ignorant, and careless, and 'out of the way'; men who will wait and watch for single souls, as the Saviour did for the woman of Samaria at the well, although she was a woman of a false theology and a broken character; men who will love and not grow cold, but who, having loved, like Jesus, will 'love to the end'.[48]

And so to recap: What precisely is that 'true standard' to which King referred at the opening of his remarks to the ordinands? Here, suggests King, comes the goal of all our theological strivings, indeed the whole point of religion in general and Christianity in particular, with a pressing relevance for those preparing to lead others to that 'true standard':

A priest will indeed require the knowledge of all theology to a certain degree . . . but the centre of it all is personal holiness. I have confined myself, brethren, on this your first gathering to this one requisite for the ministry — holiness. Whatever else may be required of learning and wisdom, and toil, *this* is essential, for 'without holiness no man can see the Lord.[49]

SPIRITUAL LIFE IS FOR EVERYBODY
IN ANY WALK OF LIFE

Although it is clear that King gave his attention, as of a special priority to the work of ministerial formation for ordinands and for the clergy in his diocese, or who came to him for spiritual counselling , nevertheless, he would have been the first to assert that:

> True holiness of life is authenticated not in some rarefied 'laboratory' of professionals, but rather in the workplace, the home, the family and communities, living out the 'trivial round, the common task.[50]

Neither is holiness of life the exclusive calling of some spiritual elite, or superhuman specimens of spirituality. We are all called to holiness, to personal conversion and transformation of life. For it is not the saints who are superhuman, so much as that the rest of us are less than human, constantly failing to realize, and falling short of our full, divinely human potential.

King would have readily applauded the words of St Francis de Sales in his *Introduction to the Devout Life*—words that could just have easily flowed from the pen of King himself:

> Nearly everyone who has written about the spiritual life has had in mind those who live apart from the world, or at least the devotion they advocate would lead to such retirement. My intention is to write for those who have to live in the world and who, according to their

state, to all outward appearances have to lead
an ordinary life; and who, often enough, will not
think of undertaking a devout life, considering
it impossible; no one, they believe, ought to
aspire to the palm of Christian piety while
surrounded by the affairs of the world.

King's call to be 'Christ-like Christians' was addressed
to all: it was simple; it was consistent:

> Our aim is nothing less than . . . the restoration
> of the image of God in which we were originally
> created. Christ has come to show us what that
> image was. 'He that hath seen me hath seen
> the Father.' Our aim, then, is to be Christ-like
> Christians.

King gave himself unstintingly to visiting his village
churches and helping them to keep the vision of the
message which he preached, because as he said:

> A church full of people, not only *saying* that
> they believe, but showing forth their faith by
> lives full of honesty, full of love, full of purity.
> This will be *far* more convincing than the
> largest library full of the oldest and cleverest
> books—the holy and devout lives of Christian
> men and women.[51]

So as King went around the little villages in his huge
and sprawling diocese of Lincoln, his gospel was the
same whether for rich or poor, for farmers, village
lads and girls, the railway men or the nurses of the
Guild of St Barnabas. Of course he would adapt the
illustrations of his gospel themes when preaching
at Confirmations or parish Visitations, all alike were

delivered with that two fold effectiveness of simplicity and depth.

'It is all very simple', as he wrote in one of his Spiritual Letters—'the love of God and love of man: That is perfection! Keep your heart with God, and then do the daily duties and He will take care of you.'[52]

Or perhaps even more simply and directly in words to his nurses in the Guild of St Barnabas: 'Hold fast to the old Faith. Teach it in love. Prove its value and power by your Christ-like lives.'[53]

The Collect for the Commemoration of Edward King on 8 March reads:

> God of peace, who gave such grace to your servant Edward King that whomever he met he drew to Christ: Fill us, we pray, with tender sympathy and joyful faith, that we also may win others to know the love that passes knowledge; through him who is the Shepherd and Guardian of our souls, Jesus Christ your Son our Lord, who is alive and reigns with you, in the unity of the Holy Spirit, one God, now and for ever. AMEN[54]

NOTES

Notes to the Introduction

1. Randolph and Townroe, *The Mind and Work of Bishop King*, London: A. R. Mowbray & Co., 1918, p. 78.
2. Rowan Williams, Foreword to Michael Marshall, *Edward King, Teacher, Bishop, Pastor, Saint*, Leominster: Gracewing, 2021.
3. George W. E Russell, *Edward King, Sixtieth Bishop of Lincoln*, London: Smith, Elder & Co., 1912, p. 55.
4. For further reading on the life of Edward King, see the Bibliography, and in particular, *Edward King: Teacher, Pastor, Bishop, Saint* by Michael Marshall, published by Gracewing, 2021.
5. G. F. Wilgress, *Edward King, Bishop of Lincoln, 1885–1910*, Lincoln: Bradley Press, *c*. 1930, p. 16.

Notes to Chapter 1

1. 'Spiritual Lives', in Edward King, *Easter Sermons*, ed. B. W. Randolph, London: A. R. Mowbray & Co., 1914, p. 44.
2. Rowan Williams, Foreword to Marshall, *Edward King*, p. xi.
3. Russell, *Edward King, Sixtieth Bishop of Lincoln*, p. 328.
4. Alister E. McGrath, *Christian Spirituality*, London: Blackwell Publishing, 1999, p. 1.
5. Rowan Williams, *Being Disciples: Essentials of the Christian Life*, London: SPCK, 2016, p. 75.
6. John D. Zizioulas, in B. McGinn and J. Meyendorff, ed., *Christian Spirituality: Origins to the Twelfth Century* (World Spirituality, vol. 16), London: Routledge & Kegan Paul, 1986, p. 27.
7. Kenneth Leech, *The Eye of the Storm: Spiritual Resources for the Pursuit of Justice*. London: Darton, Longman & Todd, 1992, pp. 3–4.
8. King, *Easter Sermons*, pp. 43–6.
9. Owen Chadwick, *The Founding of Cuddesdon*, Oxford: Oxford University Press, 1954, p. 114.
10. Stephen Platten, review of Michael Marshall's biography of Edward King, *Journal of Anglican Studies*, 2021.
11. Russell, *Edward King, Sixtieth Bishop of Lincoln*, p. 322.

[12] *Ibid.*, pp. 322–3.

[13] Edward King, *Duty and Conscience*, ed. B. W. Randolph, London: A. R. Mowbray & Co., 1911, p. 39.

[14] Russell, *Edward King, Sixtieth Bishop of Lincoln*, p. 323.

[15] Edward King, *Pastoral Lectures of Bishop Edward King*, ed. Eric Graham, London: A. R. Mowbray & Co., 1932, p. 29.

[16] Edward King, *Counsels to Nurses*, ed. E. F. Russell, London: A. R. Mowbray & Co., 1911, p. 88.

[17] King, *Duty and Conscience*, p. 16.

[18] Russell, *Edward King, Sixtieth Bishop of Lincoln*, p. 90.

[19] King, *Duty and Conscience*, p. 68.

[20] A. C. Benson, *The Life of Edward White Benson*, London: Macmillan & Co., 1899, vol. 2, p. 352.

[21] Frederick H. Borsch, 'Ye shall be Holy', in Geoffrey Rowell, ed., *Tradition Renewed: The Oxford Movement Conference Papers*, London: Darton, Longman & Todd, 1986, p. 74.

[22] Henry Scott Holland, *A Bundle of Memories*, London: Wells Gardener, Darton & Co., 1915, p. 51.

[23] J. G. Lockhart, *Cosmo Gordon Lang*, London: Hodder & Stoughton, 1949, p. 66.

[24] John A. Newton, *Search for a Saint*, London: Epworth Press, 1977, p. 105.

[25] King, *Counsels to Nurses*, p. 123.

Notes to Chapter 2

[1] King, *Easter Sermons*, p. 38.

[2] Russell, *Edward King, Sixtieth Bishop of Lincoln*, p. 304.

[3] King, *Easter Sermons*, p. 38.

[4] *Ibid.*, pp. 1–2.

[5] King, *Easter Sermons*, p. 45.

[6] *Ibid.*, p. 7.

[7] *Ibid.*, p. 8.

[8] Edward King, *Sermons and Addresses*, ed. B. W. Randolph, London: Longmans, Green & Co., p. 125.

[9] King, *Easter Sermons*, pp. 29–31.

[10] *Ibid.*, p. 41.

[11] King, *Easter Sermons*, p. 40.

[12] *Ibid.*, p. 92.

[13] *Ibid.*, p. 42.

[14] *Ibid.*, p. 54.

[15] *Ibid.*, p. 55.

[16] See Chapter 1, p. 17.

Notes

17 Russell, *Edward King, Sixtieth Bishop of Lincoln*, p. 319.
18 Edward King, *The Love and Wisdom of God*, ed. B. W. Randolph, London: Longmans, Green & Co., 1910, p. 306.
19 Rowell, *Tradition Renewed*, p. 65.
20 *Ibid..*
21 Metropolitan Ignatius of Latakia, addressing the Assembly of the World Council of Churches at Uppsala in June 1968.
22 Geoffrey Rowell, *The Vision Glorious: Themes and Personalities of the Catholic Revival in Anglicanism*, Oxford: Oxford University Press, 1983, p. 41.
23 *Ibid.*, p. 41.
24 Randolph and Townroe, *The Mind and Work of Bishop King*, pp. 26–7.
25 *Ibid.* p. 25.
26 Edward King, *Spiritual Letters*, ed. B. W. Randolph, London: A. R. Mowbray & Co., Letter IX, p. 14.

Notes to Chapter 3

1   Russell, *Edward King, Sixtieth Bishop of Lincoln*, p. 330.
2   King, *Spiritual Letters*, Letter XII, p. 18.
3   Russell, *Edward King, Sixtieth Bishop of Lincoln*, p. 330.
4   *Ibid.* p. 335.
5   Rowell, *Tradition Renewed*, p. 72.
6   King, *Spiritual Letters*, Letter XII, p. 18.
7   King, *Easter Sermons*, p. 62.
8   Russell, *Edward King, Sixtieth Bishop of Lincoln*, p. 319.
9   John V. Taylor, *The Go Between God: The Holy Spirit and the Christian Mission*, London: SCM Press, 1972, p. 17.
10 *Ibid.*
11 King, *The Love and Wisdom of God*, p. 325.
12 King *Easter Sermons*, p. 32.
13 *Ibid.*, p. 93.
14 *Ibid.*, p. 31.
15 *Ibid.*, pp. 61–2.
16 King, *The Love and Wisdom of God*, p. 321.
17 Randolph and Townroe, *The Mind and Work of Bishop King*, p. 135.
18 Alexander Schmemann, *The World as Sacrament*, London: Darton, Longman & Todd, 1966, p. 10.
19 Wilgress, *Edward King*, p. 20.
20 John William Burgon, *Inspiration and Interpretation: Seven Sermons*, Oxford & London: J. H. & James Parker, 1861, p. 46 (Sermon II).
21 Russell, *Edward King, Sixtieth Bishop of Lincoln*, p. 321.

22 *Ibid.*, p. 325.
23 King, *The Love and Wisdom of God*, pp. 312–13.
24 *Ibid.* p. 315.
25 Rowell, *Tradition Renewed*, p. 81.
26 Rowell, *The Vision Glorious*, p. 33.
27 Rowell, *Tradition Renewed*, p. 78.
28 Russell, *Edward King, Sixtieth Bishop of Lincoln*, p. 322.
29 *Ibid.*, p. 323.
30 King, *Spiritual Letters*, Letter LXVIII, p. 108.

Notes to Chapter 4

1 Randolph and Townroe, *The Mind and Work of Bishop King*, p. 27.
2 King, *Sermons and Addresses*, pp. 37–8.
3 Russell, *Edward King, Sixtieth Bishop of Lincoln*, pp. 111–12.
4 *Ibid.*, p. 222.
5 King, *Spiritual Letters*, Letter XIX, p. 30.
6 *Ibid.* Letter XV, p. 182.
7 Wilgress, *Edward King*, pp. 22–3.
8 Randolph and Townroe, *The Mind and Work of Bishop King*, pp. 11–12.
9 Adam Nicholson, *The Making of Poetry: Coleridge, the Wordsworths and their Year of Marvels*, London: William Collins, 2019, p. 15.
10 King, *Spiritual Letters*, Letter XC, p. 141.
11 King, *Easter Sermons*, pp. 49–51.
12 Jonathan Bate, *Radical Wordsworth: The Poet who Changed the World*, London: William Collins, 2020, p. 476.
13 *Ibid.*, p. 479.
14 Wilgress, *Edward King*, p. 24.
15 Rowell, *The Vision Glorious*, pp. 26–7.
16 *Ibid.*, pp. 25–6.
17 *Ibid.*, p. 26.
18 King, *Counsels to Nurses*, p. 124.
19 See Chapter 3, p. 63.
20 Richard Harries, *The One Genius: Readings through the Year with Austin Farrer*, London: SPCK, 1987, p. 50.
21 Schmemann, *The World as Sacrament*, p. 21.
22 Christine Valters Paintner, *Earth, Our Original Monastery: Cultivating Wonder and Gratitude through Intimacy with Nature*, Notre Dame, Indiana: Sorin Books, 2020, pp. 93 ff.
23 Hilarion Alfeyev, *The Spiritual World of Isaac the Syrian*, Kalamazoo: Cistercian Publications, 2000, p. 43.

Notes

24 Joachim Jeremias, *Unknown Sayings of Jesus*, trans. Reginald H Fuller, New York: Macmillan, 1957, p. 95.

25 King, *Easter Sermons*, pp. 49–51.

26 Richard Rohr, *Daily Meditations*, 28 April 2022 (email broadcast).

27 King, *Duty and Conscience*, p. 103.

28 *Ibid.*, p. 101.

29 Isaac Watts, *Discourses of the Love of God*, in *Works*, London: Longman, Hurst, Rees, Orme & Brown, Paternoster Row; Leeds: Baines, Robinson & Son, Hardcastle and Heaton. Printed by Edward Baines 1812, vol. 2, p. 526.

30 Gordon Mursell, *English Spirituality*, vol. 2: *From 1700 to the Present Day*, London: SPCK, 2008, p. 65.

31 King, *Counsels to Nurses*, pp. 49–50.

32 King, *Easter Sermons*, p. 20.

33 King, *The Love and Wisdom of God*, p. 42.

34 Rowell, *The Vision Glorious*, p. 33.

35 John Philip Newell, *Sacred Earth: Sacred Soul*, London: William Collins, 2021, p. 74.

36 *Ibid.*, p. 193.

Notes to Chapter 5

1 King, *The Love and Wisdom of God*, p. 46.

2 Russell, *Edward King, Sixtieth Bishop of Lincoln*, p. 293.

3 *Ibid.*

4 King, *The Love and Wisdom of God*, p. 46.

5 Martin Thornton, *English Spirituality*, London: SPCK, 1963, p. 36.

6 *Ibid.*, p. 77.

7 King, *Sermons and Addresses*, p. 120.

8 *Ibid.*, p. 110 ff.

9 Chadwick, *The Founding of Cuddesdon*, p. 108.

10 *Ibid.*, p. 106.

11 *Ibid.*, p. 40.

12 *Ibid.*

13 King, *Sermons and Addresses*, pp. 116–17.

14 Thornton, *English Spirituality*, p. 63.

15 *Ibid.*, pp. 63–4; cf. P. Pourrat, *Christian Spirituality*, London: Burns, Oates & Co., 1922, vol. 1, p. 185.

16 King, *The Love and Wisdom of God*, p. 72.

17 *Ibid.* p. 76.

18 Thornton, *English Spirituality*, pp. 103–4.

19 *Ibid.*, p. 96.

20 Louis Bouyer, *The Cistercian Heritage*, trans. E. Livingston, London: A. R. Mowbray & Co., 1958, p. 105.

21 King, *The Love and Wisdom of God*, p. 138.

22 *Ibid.*, pp. 227–8.

23 King, *Spiritual Letters*, Letter XXX, p. 52.

24 William Johnston, *The Inner Eye of Love: Mysticism and Religion*, London: William Collins, 1978, p. 21.

25 King, *Spiritual Letters*, Letter LXVI, p. 105.

26 *Ibid.*

27 King, *Pastoral Lectures*, p. 31.

28 Jane Shaw, *Pioneers of Modern Spirituality*, London: Darton, Longman & Todd, 2018, p. 13.

29 Dean Inge, *Christian Mysticism*, London: Methuen, 1899, p. 45.

30 King, *Counsels to Nurses*, p. 122.

31 William Johnston, *The Inner Eye of Love: Mysticism and Religion*, London: Collins, 1978, p. 29.

32 Russell, *Edward King, Sixtieth Bishop of Lincoln*, p. 86.

33 Newton, *Search for a Saint*, p. 71.

34 Russell, *Edward King, Sixtieth Bishop of Lincoln*, p. 96.

35 Lord Elton, *Edward King and Our Times*, London: Geoffrey Bles, 1958, p. 34.

36 Henry D. Rack, *Reasonable Enthusiast: John Wesley and the Rise of Methodism*, London: Epworth Press, 1989, p. 447.

37 King, *Counsels to Nurses*, p. 127.

38 *Some Maxims Gathered from the Writings of Edward King, Bishop of Lincoln*, by Canon Townroe, privately published and dedicated to the parish of St Peter-at-Gowts, Lincoln, n.d., p. 14.

39 King, *Counsels to Nurses*, p. 127.

40 Johnston, *The Inner Eye of Love*, pp. 24–5.

41 King, *Counsels to Nurses*, p. 84.

42 C. S. Lewis, 'The Weight of Glory', in *They Asked for a Paper*, London: Geoffrey Bles, 1962, pp. 196 ff.

Notes to Chapter 6

1 King, *Spiritual Letters*, Letter XX, pp. 31–2.

2 Russell, *Edward King, Sixtieth Bishop of Lincoln*, pp. 104–5.

3 *Ibid.*

4 Thornton, *English Spirituality*, p. 14.

5 Newton, *Search for a Saint*, p. 106.

6 Thornton, *English Spirituality*, pp. 48–9.

Notes

7   Newton, *Search for a Saint*, p. 44.

8   King, *The Love and Wisdom of God*, p. 46.

9   Charlie Cleverly, *The Song of Songs: Exploration the Divine Romance*, London: Hodder & Stoughton, 2015, p. 16.

10   Augustine, *Enarrationes in Psalmos*, trans. and annotated by Scholastica Hebgin and Felicitas Corrigan, vol. II, Psalms 30–7, New York: Newman Press, 1961, second discourse on Psalm 31, p. 69.

11   Augustine, *Confessions* VII.xiii.19.

12   Cleverly, *Song of Songs*, p. 14.

13   Cuddesdon College, *Cuddesdon College 1854–1929: A Record and Memorial*, Oxford: Oxford University Press, 1930, p. 52.

14   King, *The Love and Wisdom of God*, p. 138.

15   *Cuddesdon College 1854–1929*, p. 52.

16   Randolph and Townroe, *The Mind and Work of Bishop King*, p. 59.

17   *Ibid.*, p. 107.

18   *The Prayers and Meditations of Saint Anselm with the Proslogian*, trans. Sister Benedicta Ward, SLG, Harmondsworth: Penguin, 1973, p. 72.

19   *Ibid.*, p. 72.

20   Aelred of Rievaulx, *On Spiritual Friendship*, ed. Basil Pennington, OCSO, Cistercian Fathers Series, Washington, DC: Cistercian Publications, Consortium Press, 1974, p. 21.

21   *Ibid.*, pp. 21–2.

22   Scott Holland, *A Bundle of Memories*, pp. 49–50.

23   Chadwick, *The Founding of Cuddesdon*, p. 112.

24   Randolph and Townroe, *The Mind and Work of Bishop King*, p. 139.

25   Owen Chadwick, *Edward King, Bishop of Lincoln, 1885–1910*, Lincoln Minster Pamphlets, 2nd ser., 4, Friends of Lincoln Cathedral, 1968, pp. 3–4.

26   Randolph and Townroe, *The Mind and Work of Bishop King*, p. 59.

27   Philip Sheldrake, *Befriending our Desires*, London: Darton, Longman & Todd, 1994, p. 72.

28   Randolph and Townroe, *The Mind and Work of Bishop King*, p. 14.

29   Barry A. Orford, 'Edward King 1829–1910', *CR* 328, 1985.

30   King, *Spiritual Letters*, Letter LXXI, p. 111.

31   C. J. Smith, *Berkeley William Randolph: A Memoir*, Oxford: A. R. Mowbray, 1925, p. 58.

32   H. C. G. Matthew, *Gladstone 1809–1898*, Oxford: Clarendon Press, 1997, p. 93.

33   King, *Pastoral Lectures*, pp. 20–1.

34   *Ibid.*.

35   King, *Spiritual Letters*, Letter XX, p. 31.

36   Francis de Sales and Jane de Chantal, *Letters of Spiritual Direction*, trans. Peronne Marie Thibert, VHH, preface by Henri J. M. Nouwen, New York: Paulist Press, 1988, pp. 3/4.

Notes to Chapter 7

1 King, *The Love and Wisdom of God*, p. 156.
2 Thornton, *English Spirituality*, p. 51.
3 Alastair V Campbell, *Rediscovering Pastoral Care*, London: Darton, Longman & Todd, 1981, p. 5.
4 Randolph and Townroe, *The Mind and Work of Bishop King*, p. 84.
5 Russell, *Edward King, Sixtieth Bishop of Lincoln*, p. 62.
6 Newton, *Search for a Saint*, p. 62.
7 Randolph and Townroe, *The Mind and Work of Bishop King*, p. 89.
8 Russell, *Edward King, Sixtieth Bishop of Lincoln*, p. 110.
9 Randolph and Townroe, *The Mind and Work of Bishop King*, pp. 45 ff.
10 Russell, *Edward King, Sixtieth Bishop of Lincoln*, p. 57.
11 *Ibid.*, p. 55.
12 King, *Spiritual Letters*, no. VII, p. 12.
13 King, *Pastoral Lectures*, p. 32.
14 King, *Spiritual Letters*, Letter XXII, p. 35.
15 Wilgress, *Edward King*, p. 8.
16 *The Spiritual Maxims of St Francis de Sales*, ed. C. F. Kelley, London: Longmans, Green & Co., 1954, p. 124.
17 Rowell, *Tradition Renewed*, p. 73.
18 *Shrewsbury Chronicle*, 8 August 1879.
19 Randall Thomas Davidson and William Benham, *Life of Archibald Campbell Tait, Archbishop of Canterbury*, 2 vols, London: Macmillan & Co., 1891, vol. 2, p. 524.
20 Randolph and Townroe, *The Mind and Work of Bishop King*, p. 90.
21 Richard Rohr, *A Spring within Us*, London: SPCK (2018), p. 209.
22 *Ibid.*
23 Newton, *Search for a Saint*, p. 65.
24 Randolph and Townroe, *The Mind and Work of Bishop King*, pp. 69–70.
25 *Ibid.*, pp. 85–8.
26 *Ibid.*, p. 53.
27 *Ibid.*, p. 54.
28 *Ibid.*, pp. 6–7.
29 *Ibid.*, p. 53.
30 Russell, *Edward King, Sixtieth Bishop of Lincoln*, p. 56.
31 *Ibid.*, p. 27.
32 King, *Spiritual Letters*, Letter XLV, p. 72.
33 Thornton, *English Spirituality*, p. 103.
34 King, *The Love and Wisdom of God*, p. 156.
35 Aelred, *On Spiritual Friendship*, p. 11.
36 King, *Spiritual Letters*, Letter LIII, p. 86.

Notes

37   Russell, *Edward King, Sixtieth Bishop of Lincoln*, p. 279.
38   *Ibid.*, p. 280.
39   Randolph and Townroe, *The Mind and Work of Bishop King*, p. 254.
40   King, *Easter Sermons*, p. 85.
41   Francis de Sales and Jane Chantal, *Letters of Spiritual Direction*, pp. 82–3.
42   *Ibid.*, p. 51.
43   K. E. Kirk *Some Principles of Moral Theology*, London: Longmans, 1948 [1920], p. 8.
44   King, *The Love and Wisdom of God*, p. 271.
45   Thomas C. Oden, 'Freedom to Learn', a paper presented to the International Congress on Pastoral Care and Counselling, Edinburgh, 1979, as quoted in Alastair V. Campbell, *Rediscovering Pastoral care*, London: Darton Longman & Todd, 1981, p. 2.
46   Williams, Foreword to Marshall, *Edward King*.

Notes to Chapter 8

1   King, *Maxims*, p. 14.
2   Lockhart, *Cosmo Gordon Lang*, p. 77.
3   Rowan Williams *Open to Judgement: Sermons and Addresses*, London: Longman and Todd, 1994, p. 136.
4   Scott Holland, *A Bundle of Memories*, p. 61.
5   Randolph and Townroe, *The Mind and Work of Bishop King*, p. 175.
6   Pope John Paul II, Apostolic Letter, *Novo millennio ineunte*, to the Bishops, Clergy and Lay Faithful at the Close of the Great Jubilee Year, 2000, Vatican City: Case Editrice Vaticana, 2000, n. 7.
7   Scott Holland, *A Bundle of Memories*, p. 48.
8   Russell, *Edward King, Sixtieth Bishop of Lincoln*, p. 111.
9   Introduction to *Counsels to Nurses*, p. 8.
10   John O'Donohue, *Anam Cara: Spiritual Wisdom from the Celtic World*, London: Bantam Books, 1997, p. 68.
11   *Ibid.*, p. 131.
12   Collect for the Seventh Sunday after Trinity in *Book of Common Prayer*.
13   O' Donohue, *Anam Cara*, p. 136.
14   Scott Holland, *A Bundle of Memories*, p. 49.
15   King, *Duty and Conscience*, p. 93.
16   F. D. How, *Bishop Walsham How: A Memoir*, London: Isbister, 1898, p. 96.
17   Baron Friedrich von Hügel, *Essays and Addresses on the Philosophy of Religion* (1921), quoted in Church of England, *The Commemoration of Saints and Heroes of the Faith in the Anglican Communion*, London: SPCK, 1957, p. 65.
18   Chadwick, *The Founding of Cuddesdon*, p. 15.

19. *Lincoln Diocesan Magazine,* January 1887 (Lincolnshire Archives).
20. King, *Pastoral Lectures,* p. 67.
21. Rack, *Reasonable Enthusiast,* p. 88.
22. *Ibid,* p. 96.
23. Russell, *Edward King, Sixtieth Bishop of Lincoln,* p. 145.
24. Newton, *Search for a Saint,* p. 81.
25. King, *Easter Sermons,* pp. 9–10.
26. *Ibid.*
27. King, *The Love and Wisdom of God,* p. 316.
28. Francis de Sales and Jane de Chantal, *Letters of Spiritual Direction,* p. 10.
29. See Chapter 1, p. 17.
30. Francis de Sales and Jane de Chantal, *Letters of Spiritual Direction,* p. 10.
31. *Ibid.,* pp 10–11.
32. *Ibid.,* p. 79.
33. Philip Sherrard, *The Rape of Man and Nature,* Golgonooza: Suffolk Press, 1987, p. 27.
34. King, *Duty and Conscience,* p. 74.
35. King, *Easter Sermons,* p. 59.
36. *Ibid.,* p. 60.
37. *Ibid.,* p. 43.
38. *Ibid.,* p. 42.
39. Rowell, *Tradition Renewed,* p. 227.
40. Third Address, *Lambeth Conference Quiet Day, Wisdom and Love of God,* p. 322.
41. Russell, *Edward King, Sixtieth Bishop of Lincoln,* p. 212.
42. King, *Spiritual Letters,* Letter LXVIII, p. 108.
43. *Unity Begins at Home: A Report from the First British Conference on Faith and Order, Nottingham, 1964,* ed. R. E. Davies, SCM Broadsheet, vol. 5, London: SCM Press, 1964, p. 29.
44. Russell, *Edward King, Sixtieth Bishop of Lincoln,* p. 333.
45. Rowell, *Tradition Renewed,* p. 68.
46. *Ibid.,* p. 75.
47. Shaw, *Pioneers of Modern Spirituality,* p. 21.
48. King, *The Love and Wisdom of God,* pp. 266 ff.
49. *Ibid.,* pp. 268–76.
50. John Keble, *The Christian Year: Thoughts in Verse for the Sundays and Holy Days throughout the Year,* London: Church Literature Association, 1977, p. 4.
51. King, *Duty and Conscience,* pp. 10–11.
52. King, *Spiritual Letters,* Fragments: letter II, p. 176.
53. King, *Counsels to Nurses,* p. 114.
54. Collect appointed for King's *Commemoration,* 8 March; Epistle, Hebrews 13:1–8, Gospel, Matthew 9:35–7.

SELECT BIBLIOGRAPHY

WORKS OF EDWARD KING

Spiritual Letters of Edward King, D.D., ed. B. W. Randolph, London: A. R. Mowbray, 1910.

The Love and Wisdom of God: A Collection of Sermons, ed. B. W. Randolph, London, New York, Bombay, Calcutta: Longmans, 1910.

Sermons and Addresses, ed. B. W. Randolph, London, New York, Bombay, Calcutta: Longmans, 1911.

Easter Sermons Preached in Lincoln Cathedral, ed. B. W. Randolph, London: A. R. Mowbray, 1914.

Meditations on the Last Seven Words of Our Lord Jesus Christ, London: A. R. Mowbray, 1910.

Pastoral Lectures of Bishop Edward King, ed. Eric Graham, London & Oxford: A. R. Mowbray, 1932.

Counsels to Nurses: Addresses and Letters to the Guild of St Barnabas for Nurses, ed. E. F. Russell, London: A. R. Mowbray, 1911.

Duty and Conscience, Addresses Given in Parochial Retreats at St Mary Magdalen's, Paddington, ed. B. W. Randolph, London, 1911.

Some Maxims Gathered from the Writings of Edward King, Bishop of Lincoln, by Canon Townroe, privately published and dedicated to the parish of St Peter-at-Gowts, Lincoln, n.d.

ARCHIVAL SOURCES

Lincolnshire Archives at St Rumbold Street, Lincoln, LN2 5AB for copies of *Diocesan Magazine* (1886–8; 1889–91; 1910–11): *A Notebook of King's Days at Oriel and Summaries of Sermons*. Also, *Visitation Records* as well as a collection of letters from William Bright. In 1967, Geoffrey Larken deposited a valuable collection of King's papers, originally from H. R. Bramley and Canon Hubert Larken.

Keble College, Oxford: Liddon Papers and Bright Papers.

Pusey House, Oxford: A selection of unpublished letters of King, also A Minute Book and Records of The Brotherhood of the Holy Trinity.

Pusey House, Oxford: Liddon Manuscripts, The Liddon Diaries.

Bishop's House, Ely: Conferences of East Anglia Bishops, minutes of meetings from 1889.

Church of St Mary, Stone, Kent: The Personal Journal of Archdeacon King—'The Dark Green Ledger'.

PUBLISHED STUDIES OF EDWARD KING

Chadwick, Owen, *Edward King Bishop of Lincoln, 1885–1910*, Lincoln Minster Pamphlets, second series, no. 4, Lincoln, 1968.

Chadwick, Owen, *The Founding of Cuddesdon*, Oxford: Oxford University Press, 1954.

Cuddesdon College 1854–1929: A Record and Memorial, Oxford, 1930.

Elton, Lord, *Edward King and Our Times*, London: Geoffrey Bles, 1958.

Marshall, Michael, *Edward King: Teacher, Pastor, Bishop, Saint*, Leominster: Gracewing, 2021.

Newton, John A., *Search for a Saint: Edward King*, London: Epworth Press, 1977.

Randolph, B. W., and J. W. Townroe, *The Mind and Work of Bishop King*, London & Milwaukee: A. R. Mowbray, 1918.

Russell, G. W. E., *Edward King, Sixtieth Bishop of Lincoln: A Memoir*, London: Smith, Elder & Co., 1912.

Wilgress, G. F., *Edward King, Bishop of Lincoln 1885–1910*, London: Bradley Press, n.d.

OTHER WORKS CONSULTED

Bundock, John F., *Old Leigh: A Pictorial History*, Phillimore, 1978.

Clark, Kenneth, *'The Lantern of Kent'. A Guide to the History of St Mary the Virgin, Stone*, Gavin Martin, Colournet Ltd, 2015.

Francis de Sales and Jane de Chantal, *Letters of Spiritual Direction*, The Classics of Western Spirituality, New York: Paulist Press, 1988.

Select Bibliography

Kirk, K. E., *The Vision of God* (abridged edition), Cambridge: James Clarke & Co., 1934.

Outler, Albert C., *John Wesley's Sermons*, Nashville: Abingdon Press, 1991.

Rack, Henry D., *Reasonable Enthusiast. John Wesley and the Rise of Methodism*, London: Epworth Press, 1989.

Rowell, Geoffrey, *The Vision Glorious: Themes and Personalities of the Catholic Revival in Anglicanism*, Oxford: Oxford University Press, 1983.

Rowell, Geoffrey, ed., *Tradition Renewed: The Oxford Movement Conference Papers*, London: Darton, Longman & Todd, 1986.

Scott Holland, Henry, *A Bundle of Memories*, London: Wells Gardner, Darton & Co., 1915.

INDEX

Index

Index

Wilberforce, William 204

William of St Thierry 119, 120, 142, 143

Williams, Rowan, Archbishop 7, 9, 11, 18, 193, 197

Wordsworth, Christopher, Bishop 191

Wordsworth, William 86, 87, 89, 90, 91, 99, 191

Lightning Source UK Ltd.
Milton Keynes UK
UKHW012132291222
414424UK00002B/15